THE SKEPTIC AND THE RABBI

Published 2017

Printed in the United States of America

Print ISBN: 978-1-63152-302-1
E-ISBN: 978-1-63152-303-8
Library of Congress Control Number: 2017938479

For information, address:
She Writes Press
1563 Solano Ave #546
Berkeley, CA 94707

Cover design © Julie Metz, Ltd./metzdesign.com
Formatting by Katherine Lloyd/theDESKonline.com

She Writes Press is a division of SparkPoint Studio, LLC.

Names and identifying characteristics have been changed to protect the privacy of certain individuals.

THE SKEPTIC AND THE RABBI

FALLING IN LOVE WITH FAITH

A MEMOIR

JUDY GRUEN

She Writes Press, a BookSparks imprint
A Division of SparkPointStudio, LLC.

Also by Judy Gruen

Till We Eat Again: A Second Helping

MBA Admissions for Smarties: The No-Nonsense Guide to Acceptance at Top Business Schools (with Linda Abraham)

The Women's Daily Irony Supplement

Carpool Tunnel Syndrome: Motherhood as Shuttle Diplomacy

This book is dedicated to the memory of my grandparents

Rabbi Bernard Cohen, PhD

Ethel Goldman Cohen

Herbert Theodore Rosenfeld

Cecelia Rosenfeld, MD

Table of Contents

FOREWORD

by Michael Medved

THERE'S A COMMON TALMUDIC TERM–*Nogaya B'Davar*–that ought to disqualify me immediately from attempting an appropriate foreword for Judy Gruen's fine book.

A *Nogaya B'Davar* is an interested party, a concerned individual with an unmistakable stake in some enterprise or dispute. If you're *Nogaya B'Davar* you can't pretend to be impartial and I can't possibly feign impartiality to the events and arguments that Judy describes so vividly in these pages.

My wife Diane and I played a small personal role in Judy's journey toward Orthodox Jewish commitment, and we participated in the frenzied celebration of her fairy tale (or *frummy* tale) wedding some quarter century ago. Her husband Jeff succeeded me as president of the California congregation I co-founded, and he counts as one of the most honorable and universally admired individuals I've ever encountered. The pride I feel in Judy's eloquent description of her spiritual and intellectual development is as much personal as it is professional.

Yet even those who have never met the Gruens will come away from this reading experience with the sense that you can now number them among your intimate friends. Through the intimacy and force of her writing, Judy presents family members and friends that I don't know personally with the same vivifying affection with which she describes characters I've known for many years.

This marvelous book should connect with the widest possible readership–ferociously religious or fervently secular; Jewish, Christian or humanist; baby boomer, Gen X-er or Millennial. Unlike other conversion stories, Judy stresses the fact that making a religious commitment need not involve a transformation that is immediate or total. A spiritual awakening, a sense of adventure, and a near idyllic romance may have led her to a new life as a religious Jew, but they never created a wholly new, unrecognizable personality. The old Judy is still very much there, capable of looking with bemused skepticism at the fulfilling Orthodox existence she establishes for herself and her family.

Her example makes a crucial point for all people of faith, and for those friendly doubters or deniers with a sincere desire to understand them. When an individual pursues a new religious path, she may hear angels singing or bells ringing, but it's the beginning, not the end, of her most important story. Any seeker who longs for a climactic resolution of all doubts and divisions, capped with the words "and they lived happily ever after," won't find such trite conclusions in religious congregations of any denomination. That's especially true for Jews, who take seriously the teaching that our forefather Jacob earned the name "Israel" by wrestling with God. Like so many serious Jews of recent generations, Judy keeps alive within her household the spirit of both sets of grandparents–the cheerfully disbelieving secularists alongside the philosophically rigorous religious believers. Most Jewish families in the United States can identify relatives or ancestors who felt the powerful claims of religious observance, as well as others who preferred to devote their Friday nights to Woody Allen movies or sweet-and-sour pork at Cantonese restaurants.

To an undeniable degree, Judy's relationship with Judaism comes across as a serious romance, but one that raises as many new life questions as it settles. The call to "rules, rituals, and restraint" that she associates with Rabbi Daniel Lapin, her teacher (and mine), don't bring an end to thinking and choosing but provide a means to think more deeply and choose more richly.

In reliving this story through these pages, I'm reminded of the immortal epigraph to the 1910 novel, *Howard's End,* by the supremely eloquent English, non-Jewish novelist E. M. Forster. "Only connect," the great storyteller exhorts his readers, and Judy Gruen hopes to encourage the same sort of connections: between romantic partners, family members, present and distant generations, believers and scoffers, logic and passion, author and readers and, ultimately, unavoidably, between God and his people.

Introduction

I was just seconds from a clean getaway.

I ducked out early from a weekend writers' conference on Saturday night, right after *Shabbos* ended. My daughter was leaving for camp the next morning, and I drove back to L.A. from Ventura County to help her finish packing. Just as the hotel elevator doors began to close, a long arm thrust itself forward, wrenching them open again. Another conference attendee entered. With one swift glance, he assessed my belongings on the luggage cart.

I braced myself. I knew what was coming.

Most of my items were unremarkable: a small suitcase, cooler bag, and a book bag. But the cart also held a tall red and white cardboard box, printed with the peculiar description KOSHER LAMP, in nearly marquee-sized, bold, capital letters. You didn't need a journalism degree to have to wonder about that.

"What is a kosher lamp?" my fellow traveler asked, one eyebrow arched. His tone was slightly mocking, and I was pretty sure that we were members of the same tribe. I groaned inwardly. It was impossible to offer an instant and satisfying answer to his completely reasonable question. I felt like the famous Jewish sage Hillel, who had once been challenged by a skeptic to explain the entire Torah while standing on one foot.

"The lamp has a movable cover so you can close or open the light over *Shabbos*," I explained, already falling way short of the Hillel standard. And what was taking this elevator so long to descend two floors? Was it stuck or something? "This way I can use the light without turning on any switches."

"And what do you think the Talmud would say about that?" he parried, smirking.

Oh, the chutzpah of my people! Only Jews are nervy enough to challenge other Jews–even total strangers–about their religious observance or lack thereof.

As we entered the lobby, I looked him straight in the eye and said, "Given that the Talmud was written by our most brilliant Torah scholars, I think that they'd say it takes a real *Yiddishe kop* (a smart Jewish mind) to think of something so inventive!" Pleased with my response, I held my head high and steered my cart out of the elevator, out of the hotel, and to my car.

As I was buckling my seat belt, I was surprised to see the man crossing the parking lot toward me. I lowered the window as he approached. With a much kinder expression on his face, he said, "Drive safe and have a good week."

I smiled and wished him the same. I was happy that he offered such a thoughtful gesture after our awkward encounter, which left me frustrated and annoyed. I figured that he had written me off as a fanatic solely because of my admittedly odd "kosher lamp," but he knew absolutely nothing else about me, and I didn't want to be summarized or labeled so blithely. How could I possibly have explained in one moment the magic of *Shabbos*, a day where we stop frantically "doing" to enjoy the serenity of "being?" How could I have begun to explain that the laws, even those as "small" as not turning on or off a light switch, add integrity and spiritual depth to Shabbos? In modern parlance, Shabbos is about being mindful, both of God and of oneself.

I resented what I assumed to be the man's negative attitude toward me, but I also understood it. Born in 1960, I was marinated in the countercultural environment that exploded in that decade and permeated the seventies, when I was a teenager. Truth be told, for years I drove around with a "Question Authority" bumper sticker on my car. Not until my mid-twenties did I decide to explore–reluctantly (and almost covertly)–what the Torah said, as taught by Orthodox-educated teachers.

I also considered myself a feminist and still held on to hazy romantic notions that this made me a bit countercultural, something I considered a slightly exalted thing. It came as a bit of a shock to discover that in an increasingly coarse and secular culture, choosing to live a Torah-based life was actually the countercultural choice.

This memoir is my answer to the man in the elevator. It is not a sugar-coated fluffy paean to the joys of religious observance. It's a real story about a real struggle, the most wrenchingly difficult decision of my life but also the best; one that has yielded blessings beyond my imagination. It's also about the legacy and impact of my grandparents, a love story between my husband and me, and even, yes, a love story between me and my faith.

Chapter 1

WEDDING DAY

JULY 12, 1987

OH MY GOD! I'M GETTING MARRIED in less than two hours–Orthodox-style.

I'm excited and scared and happy, all at the same time. Good thing I am distracted by watching the makeup artist as she smooths a cool moisturizer over my face and neck, making me look as beautiful as a scared and happy bride should look.

She had arrived with a shockingly heavy arsenal of lotions, creams, thin and fat brushes, small and large sponges, eyeliners in a dozen hues, and a rainbow coalition of eye shadows and blushers. Two sets of drawers in her case were crammed exclusively with lip liners, lipsticks, and glosses. Surgeons in the operating room don't require this much equipment.

Within the hour I'll be ready for the camera's flashing lights, photographers following me as if I'm a celebrity. Wait, today I *am* a celebrity: I'm a bride! And now that I have recovered from my self-inflicted near-fainting spell early this morning, and shaken off the momentary guilt that I broke the fast that Jeff and I were supposed to keep until after the wedding ceremony, I am calm and happy. Holly, my *shomeret*, the friend I asked to "protect" me during the twenty-four hours before the wedding, slept over with me in Jeff's and my new condo last night. This morning, she carefully packed my wedding dress into the back seat of her yellow VW bug, packed me into the front, and chauffeured me to the Hyatt Hotel. As we buckled up, my new friends John and Carol stood right outside the car, clapping and singing "Od Yishama" a lively, traditional Jewish wedding song. John and Carol also belong to my new synagogue, and were married just a few months earlier. Jeff and I like them very much and are happy they are our next-door neighbors.

The makeup artist asks, "Do you like the color of this blush? If not, I can change it." Frankly, everything she is doing looks good to me. And what do I know? At twenty-seven this is the first time I have ever had my makeup professionally done, not counting the time I was made to look like Grandmother Tzeitel from *Fiddler on the Roof* in a high school play at the synagogue. (I got the role because it was the only one in the show where a bad voice was an asset.) Sitting in my white hotel robe, I give this woman carte blanche to make me up to look lovely, but not overdone. My typical makeup routine is minimal, just a little mascara and lipstick. Today, I'm loving this once-in-a-lifetime attention to getting made up. Wow, this mascara is great. I better ask for the name of it. It seems like it would never clump.

Mom is seated nearby, watching. She is beautiful in her light-lavender beaded gown, her makeup accentuating her lovely skin and light brown eyes, her perfectly coiffed jet-black hair like a crown upon her head. Mom's expression is classic for her: pleased yet guarded. I understand why. I am the youngest of her three children, and my brother, Allan, died eighteen years earlier in a car accident. That shocking loss devastated us all, and Dad's heartbreak remains raw. So my happiness today is not only for myself; it's so much for

Mom and Dad, who have a *simcha* to celebrate. Of course, Allan is never far from my thoughts. I cannot imagine how urgently or often my parents' hearts are roiled by the long-ago traumatic loss of their firstborn, their only son.

Mom has remained remarkably sturdy over the years. She personifies the Jewish wisdom that advises, "Say little but do much." It's funny, but even as an adult I can't say I know her intimately. She is very private, but many people count themselves among her close friends and she is universally adored. When Mom's on the phone with friends, I notice that she listens more than talks, which taught me how to be a good friend. Mom's at her most bubbly with her best friend, the wisecracking Eleanor, who loves to tell ribald jokes. Mom personally would never tell such jokes, but when Eleanor tells them Mom is in stitches.

People trust Mom for her dignity and discretion. For example, for years she worked as the executive secretary for the rabbi of one of the largest synagogues in Los Angeles. When the rabbi resigned under a cloud of scandal involving an illicit relationship with a congregant, almost everyone was shocked. But Liebe Rosenfeld had known all about it, her lips sealed. Mom's loyalty always remained with the rabbi.

I knew Mom worried a bit about the way I seemed to be following Jeff into a Jewish Orthodox future. She visualized a life for me that involved a strictly kosher kitchen, complete with two sets of dishes (not including another two sets for Passover); walking to shul (synagogue) on Saturdays; higher necklines, lower hemlines, and most likely a minivan to accommodate a passel of kids. Unsure how to broach her concerns that I would become an overworked wife and mother, though, Mom instead lobbed the occasional verbal grenade.

After all, I had been the noisily liberal daughter, so concerned about politics when I was growing up that in 1972, at twelve years old, I insisted she drive me after school to the nearby McGovern presidential campaign office several times a week so I could stuff mailers and answer phones. I was an indefatigable McGovern campaigner, standing with my best friend Nancy in our neon orange McGovern '72 T-shirts outside the local supermarket on weekends, trying to persuade shoppers to vote for the Democrat Senator from South Dakota. When Senator McGovern made an appearance at our synagogue in North Hollywood, California, I pushed my way through the crowd to shake his hand, which I tried not to wash for three days as a sign of true loyalty. I was heartbroken on election eve when McGovern's poll numbers remained grim. I ran out for some last-minute door-to-door campaigning, but all my exertions proved too little, too late.

I was the daughter who stood on Sproul Plaza at UC Berkeley, shouting to all and sundry that they should contribute to Oxfam, an organization devoted to combating world hunger, in my attention-getting costume of a washing machine box-cum-giant charity box. (My roommate Miriam put me up to this, but I was more than happy to play the role.) I was the daughter who had a little painted sign in my apartment that read, "She who waits for the knight in shining armor picks up after the horse." I had only recently let my subscription to *Ms. Magazine* lapse.

So I sympathize with Mom's guarded nervousness. I myself had been so skittish of this entire kosher enterprise that for two years I spent the better part of my evenings with Jeff in debate sessions, in which I tried to prove that the Torah was sexist and outdated and he tried to prove me wrong. Fun dates, right? But it was also obvious that Jeff was the kind of man I wanted as a husband: hardworking and kind, sensitive and funny, honest and sincere. He blended a serious life purpose with appropriate light-heartedness, and I respected his quest to build a life not just of material security, but of spiritual substance. I, personally, hadn't given the idea of spiritual substance through Jewish practice much thought, but it quickly struck me as being worthy of consideration. Mom and Dad saw Jeff's potential as a good husband for me, and besides, my "sell-by" date was looming. So he was Orthodox; there were worse things!

According to prevailing Orthodox custom, Jeff and I have not seen each other for the last week before the wedding, nor spoken for the past three days. As I had done with many other new-to-me Orthodox customs, I protested at first. Why should we have any boundaries in seeing each other so close to the wedding? But now that I have lived through the pre-wedding week, I'm glad we adhered to the practice. I was full of angst yesterday at my *Shabbos Kallah* reception given by the women of the shul in my honor, and this morning only the intervention of my downstairs neighbor kept me from passing out. In light of all this, the separation now strikes me as brilliant. Jeff didn't need to see either of these episodes, and if he had private last-minute jitters of his own, I sure didn't want to know about them either. I began to understand why ignorance can be bliss.

Jeff had been nervous on the night he proposed, much to my consternation. But in the week before the wedding we switched roles: Jeff's happiness and confidence surged, while fear coursed through my veins. Over a courtship that lasted two-and-a-half years, we had discussed what our religious life would look like over and over and over. We had it mostly figured out. Now I worried anew: What if I didn't like living an Orthodox lifestyle? What if I really did lose all my secular friends, whom I feared would never understand my decision?

It is too late for all that Monday-morning quarterbacking now. The makeup artist is reinforcing the lip liner and making subtle changes to the eye shadow. Frankly, I look too pretty to back out now! Mom reports that Jeff looks very handsome and happy in his new black suit from Nordstrom, a white carnation boutonniere firmly pinned just above his heart.

"Beautiful!" Mom beams, and as I examine my reflection in the mirror from several angles, I agree. Mom holds my dress as I step into it and she zips me up. We were thrilled when I found this dress, an off-the-rack tea-length gown that cost less than most of my friends were spending on their veils alone. I've never been one for frills, and this simple lace dress is perfect, not too poufy or ornate. It doesn't have a train, so I won't worry about tripping over it. Though I had been a chubby kid, I was happy to be holding steady at a size eight, and finally felt about seventy percent comfortable in my own skin. Speaking of skin, I knew I was showing more of it than nearly all the other married women in my new religious social sphere. (I had seen their wedding photos.) I had agreed to a compromise neckline with Robin, who organized many weddings for this community and who had told me when I first showed her my dress that it was very pretty, *so pretty*, but it could use a little bit more coverage in front. Grudgingly, I let Robin take me to a dressmaker who had a brisk business in fabric remediation on wedding dresses that divulged too much for Orthodox brides. The seamstress added a few inches of lace, making it barely kosher, but Robin let it go, and I felt I had won an important victory.

Robin knocks on the door, all smiles, saying it's time to go downstairs for the *bedecken* ceremony. At the *bedecken*, I sit in a throne-like chair, my mother and Jeff's mother, Laura, seated on either side of me. Dozens of guests wait in line to greet me and offer blessings, and I feel regal. Time evaporates as I hear the murmuring of dozens of conversations around me as the pre-wedding reception plays out. Before I know it, I hear the musicians striking up a rousing, can't-help-but-clap-your-hands-and-bob-your-head rendition of "Od Yishama," the clarinet piercing the air. I can barely contain the emotions swelling inside me, and I try not to cry my makeup off.

The music grows louder and closer as my smiling groom is escorted toward me, linking arms with our respective fathers, with a larger circle of men dancing joyously around the three of them. I see my husband-to-be and feel a thrill. He looks so handsome! The air in the room sizzles with the energy of the moment. Jeff purposefully climbs the steps of the riser where I sit enthroned and gently lowers the veil over my face. This *bedecken* ceremony is based on the Biblical story of Jacob, who was tricked into marrying Leah when he intended to marry her younger sister Rachel, the woman he loved. Ever since, Jewish grooms get a look-see at their brides to ensure there is no last-minute bait-and-switch. My father blesses me, too, which just about does me in, because Dad has not been on speaking terms with God since Allan died and I do not think I have ever even heard him utter a blessing in his life.

After the *bedecken*, Robin ushers guests to their seats so we can get married already. Standing with my parents, my tummy is doing flips and I feel I am having an out-of-body experience. Is this what intense fear is like, or incalculable joy?

Oh my God! I'm getting married in a few minutes–Orthodox-style.

Chapter 2

THE GRANDPARENTS I HAVE TO THANK

1965 - 1975

If I had not been concentrating so hard just putting one foot in front of the other as I stepped tentatively down the aisle toward my future, I probably would have remembered to offer a thankful tribute to my grandparents up in heaven. Cece and Papa Rosenfeld, my paternal grandparents, are undoubtedly shaking their heads, aghast at my decision to "get holy." Nana and Papa Cohen, my mother's parents, are surely reaching for the three-ply celestial hankies to dry their copious tears of joy. All of them long departed, my wildly contrasting sets of grandparents influenced me far more than any of them realized. As much as I loved them all, these parallel worldviews created agonies for me during my courtship with Jeff as I wrestled with the decision over whether to become more religiously observant.

Lots of Jewish kids from my generation had parents like Nana and Papa, both immigrants from Eastern Europe. Each had traveled alone to flee the barbarous anti-Semitism of Eastern Europe in the early 20th century, eager for the safety and freedom promised in the so-called *goldene medina,* the "golden land" that America promised to become for millions of oppressed immigrants. How must my Nana have felt at only sixteen years old, speaking only Yiddish and Russian, and leaving her mother and sister behind in Kiev? The young Ethel Goldman had accepted her father's invitation to join him in San Francisco, but her mother and sister chose to stay behind, opting for the known dangers in Ukraine to the unknown dangers of a new, strange country where many Jews who had arrived on its shores easily shucked off most of their religious commitment. I pictured my teenaged grandmother standing on that deck in 1921, watching the shore slowly disappear, and wondering whether she would ever see her beloved family members again.

Papa Cohen got out of Poland through a minor miracle. He had already been conscripted into the Polish Army, where an officer offered him freedom in exchange for a volume of poetry in Papa's possession. So at twenty-two, faster than he could say *Na razie*, Papa packed his suitcase and booked passage to cross the Atlantic, also leaving his family and hometown of Sokoly behind.

Papa's first shock upon reaching his new land was to have his name unceremoniously changed at Ellis Island. He had arrived as Beryl Konopioty (Kah-nah-*pya*-tee), but this was a name considered too tongue-twisting for the immigration officers, and when his papers were stamped he was suddenly Bernard Cohen. Of course, Papa didn't dare question the intimidating bureaucrat but the change upset my grandfather deeply. A Kohain is a member of the priestly class of Jews descended from Moses's brother Aaron. Jews who are also Kohanim have a special status, including particular ritual obligations. (Think of the phrase "the big Kahuna" and you'll know where it comes from.) Upon meeting Papa, Jews often asked if he was indeed a Kohain, and I would hear him sigh with not a little exasperation.

"No, I'm a Yisrael," he repeatedly explained, referring to his lineage as "just" that of the more numerous, less distinguished community of Israel. "Dey changed my name at Ellis Island."

Nana and Papa were my religious grandparents, their presence a bulwark against a steep, perhaps irreversible slide toward total assimilation in my family. Papa Cohen was a man on the go, busy every moment I saw him. He and Nana spent a lot of time in our house, and Papa was usually sitting at the dining room table studying a weighty tome of the Talmud, written in both Hebrew and Aramaic. Or, he'd be reading the Yiddish newspaper, the *Forvertz*, or writing one of the innumerable articles he wrote for the Jewish press. He was a founding director of the Bureau of Jewish Education in Los Angeles and served as a judge in the Jewish religious court, the *Beit Din*, of the Conservative movement. Though raised in an Orthodox home in Europe, Papa had a modernizing streak as well. He became ordained as a rabbi in the Conservative movement, which tried to forge a middle ground between the strictures of traditional Orthodoxy and the radical liberalization of the Reform Movement.

Papa clearly saw that for all his commitment to creating a more open-minded Jewish practice that was still ardently faithful to Jewish values, assimilation among Jews in America was on a frighteningly fast trajectory. Despite his passionate activism on behalf of after-school Jewish education, only two of his five grandchildren attended Hebrew School. I frequently thought how disappointing this must have been for him and Nana. I admired Papa's status as an accomplished man of renown in the Jewish community, but his seriousness made me feel like a slacker. He'd come from the dining room to the living room and see my sister and me watching television, stand there looking stern for a few seconds and pronounce, "A vaste of time!" as if our watching TV was a personal affront. Then Papa would purposefully stride out of the house for another appointment with a congregant or committee meeting.

Nana was the quintessential *balabusta*, a traditional Jewish wife, mother and grandmother, devoted first, last and always to taking care of her family. She kept house, shopped, cooked, undoubtedly counseled some congregants' wives, taught Hebrew School, and in her middle years, earned a real estate license to supplement Papa's modest income. While I was growing up she often said, "Sveetheart, I'm saving my pennies to go and visit Israel." And she did. I admired her old-world thrift, as well as her indefatigable determination.

In wild contrast, my dad's father, Herbert Theodore Rosenfeld, was a first-generation American, a cigar-smoking, worldly man of business whose commitment to the spread of atheism and to practical jokes nearly equaled Papa Cohen's commitment to the spread of Jewish education. No doubt, there were times when just as Papa Cohen was adjudicating a court case in the *Beit Din* according to Jewish law, Papa Rosenfeld was out stumping on behalf of the American Humanist Association, campaigning for atheism, nuclear non-proliferation, and less publicly, according to some family members, Communism.

I often stayed overnight at Papa and Cece Rosenfeld's house on the weekends, and Papa would show me his latest acquisitions of toys and practical jokes: trick cards, a new Jack-in-the-box, a "dribble glass" that leaked, and a simple painting of some straight lines he hired an adolescent boy to paint and was trying to sell for some crazy amount of money. He had the boy sign the painting "Ruoy Stun"– "Your Nuts" spelled backward. I would wake in the morning to the aroma of bacon, which Papa sizzled for breakfast in a heavy cast iron skillet.

I'd often stare in fascination at the little plate of ham in their fridge, tantalizingly *treyf* (unkosher), covered with plastic wrap. "Come on, taste me! I dare you!" I heard a mocking voice in my head. I loved the salty, crunchy taste of bacon, but somehow, I found the idea of ham to be somehow even too *treyf* for me–beyond the pale. But its close proximity fascinated me. One day, almost in slow motion, I reached my hand toward that little plate of ham in the fridge, my heart beating quickly. I lifted the plastic wrap, tore off a tiny corner of the forbidden meat, and put it in my mouth. I couldn't stand it. This was a relief, as my *treyf* eating at Cece and Papa's house would be limited to beef and bacon–hold the ham would be my motto.

My grandmothers were just as entertainingly opposite. While Nana was bringing Papa another cup of tea and a slice of angel food cake as he wrote and read, Cece was dashing from patient to patient in her office, wearing a heavily starched white lab coat, embroidered with "Cecelia Rosenfeld, MD" on the pocket. Cece was Papa Rosenfeld's second wife, but she was the woman I considered every inch my grandmother. She was a medical radical, a female physician in an era when women MDs were a rarity. Even more extraordinary, Cece had renounced her allopathic medical practice to study homeopathy and acupuncture. I spent many a Saturday morning in her office in Westwood Village, watching with awe and pride as my grandmother prescribed the sweet and tiny homeopathic tablets to restore what she called homeostasis. I wasn't only her granddaughter, but a patient as well, and though I hated it when she stuck the fine acupuncture needles in me to get rid of an ear infection or virus, I couldn't exactly refuse.

Cece's popularity as a holistic physician in upscale West Los Angeles in the 1950s and 1960s attracted a loyal following of celebrities, artists, authors, and bohemians, and I was on the lookout for some of her famous patients. Barely five feet, two inches, blue-eyed and with soft brown curls, Cece was as tender and doting as any grandparent could be. Unlike Nana Cohen, whose conversation focused most often on all the things she worried about, including Papa and how hard he worked, my mother and how hard she worked, my siblings and cousins and how much she wanted us to grow up to be good Jews, Cece talked to me about all kinds of *ideas*. She discussed possible career paths for me when I grew up, and predicted that I would become a writer. She talked about one day taking me to Europe, as she and Papa had done with my brother, Allan, and later, my sister, Sharon. I felt sorry for Cece because she didn't have children of her own, so I felt it my duty to make sure she understood that I felt myself her granddaughter in every way. I did this by calling her nearly every day, spending many weekends with her and Papa at their home in a secluded cul-de-sac in Pacific Palisades, and letting her stick her acupuncture needles in me, even my head.

It was one of the ongoing thrills of my childhood to brag about "my grandmother, the doctor," a fact that induced shock and sometimes disbelief in the 1960s. When I boasted about Cece in kindergarten, my teacher, Miss Flanagan, accused me of lying.

"Everyone knows that ladies aren't doctors," Miss Flanagan said sternly, her foot-high bouffant hairdo mercilessly adding to her already towering stature. I was outraged. Why, just a few days before I had been chatting up patients in Cece's waiting room along with Papa, who served as Cece's receptionist. It was the first time in my life I had been accused of lying to anyone, except for the time I lied to Dad when I denied any knowledge of the missing goldfish from the small mayonnaise jar in my room. I was too afraid to confess that I had, after repeated attempts, picked it up by the tail, only to have it wriggle free and fall behind the dresser. Aside from that, my truthfulness was unimpeachable. The next morning, I stood triumphant next to Miss Flanagan as my mother cleared my name. I wondered why it was so hard for people to accept the idea of a lady doctor.

Friday evening at sundown ushered in the Sabbath, *Shabbes*, as Nana and Papa pronounced it. Often, we ate *Shabbos* dinner with Nana and Papa Cohen either at our home in Van Nuys, or their home in North Hollywood, about a fifteen-minute drive away. Shabbos was special, a day when strictly speaking, Jews were not supposed to do things like go shopping, watch TV, or even drive. But as Conservative Jews, Nana and Papa would drive to and from the synagogue. The rest of my family treated Friday night and Saturday as regular days, only with better dinners.

The Shabbos table at our home, or Nana's, had a crisp white tablecloth on it, and the good dishes. Mom and Nana would light two candles each in their Shabbos candlesticks, then wave their hands in a circular motion three times before covering their eyes and making the blessing in Hebrew that ushered in the day of rest. I enjoyed watching them do this, and assumed when I grew up I'd also light Shabbos candles, too. Two fresh, soft loaves of braided challah bread lay under the decorated challah cover, which Papa sliced with a special long, shiny knife, after making the kiddush blessing over the sweet Manischewitz wine. I admired how Papa always stood straight and, it seemed, with pride, wearing his Shabbos suit and reciting the kiddush in Hebrew. Then he quietly dashed from the dining room to the kitchen to pour water over his hands, two times for each hand, for the ritual washing before making the blessing over the challah. Shabbos dinner was always tasty, if not inventive: we almost always had chicken soup with matzo balls or noodles, baked chicken, green beans or carrots, and rice from a boxed mix loaded with enough salt to satisfy even the sodium-craving Rosenfeld palate.

After dinner, Mom, Nana, Papa, and I would drive over to the synagogue for services. Dad's religion was the UCLA Bruins, so he stayed home and watched whatever sports game might be on, or else a detective show. Allan and Sharon were busy with friends. I liked going to shul, even though I found the archaic English translations almost as obscure as the Hebrew. I did like the prayers that the congregation sang out loud, the feeling of community of seeing so many familiar faces, and the rabbi's sermon. He always started with a pretty good joke, and his background in theater had given him an outstanding sense of timing.

The service got better as it got close to the end, and after singing "Adon Olam," the final prayer we all sang together, Rabbi Rothblum would stand toward the edge of the stage, or *bimah,* spread his arms out over the congregation, and with his eyes closed, recite a blessing over all of us:

May the Almighty bless you and keep you.
May He shine His face upon you and be gracious toward you.
May He turn His face toward you and establish peace for you.

I just loved that. My conception of God was at best hazy, but I was pretty sure that Rabbi Rothblum must be on good terms with Him, and that God would hear that blessing and say, "Got it," or something to that effect. At the dessert reception after the service, or *oneg Shabbos,* I demonstrated a zeal for running that would have stunned my PE teacher as I sprinted past the slower, elderly people and lunged for a brownie. Sinking my full-metal-jacketed teeth into the densely fudgy extravagance, I finally had a true religious experience.

Cece and Papa Rosenfeld were never at our Shabbos table. In fact, their antipathy toward religion made it hard to have a lot of inclusive family gatherings. After a disastrous Passover seder when I was about seven, those attempts to have family events with both sets of grandparents ceased entirely.

Nana and Papa Cohen always hosted Passover seder, and that year, they invited Cece and Papa Rosenfeld also. This was quite a gamble, given Papa Rosenfeld's outspoken atheism and penchant for making jokes about religion. Cece was unapologetically agnostic, and anyway, what would Nana serve a health-conscious vegetarian at the seder? Nana's Passover menu was chicken soup, brisket, and kugels. Despite my Rosenfeld grandparents' total lack of interest in the quaint rituals involved in the annual retelling the story of the Jews' exodus from slavery in Egypt, they didn't want to appear ungracious and accepted the invitation.

The Passover seder may be the most strategically planned event on the entire Jewish calendar. Joshua's conquest of the Land of Israel probably required less plotting and organization than that involved with your average kosher Passover week. It certainly involved a lot less shopping! Passover, or Pesach, celebrates God's deliverance of the Jews after two hundred and ten years of brutal slavery in Egypt. It is an article of faith that this was a personal deliverance by God Himself, who then led the Jews out of Egypt and, circuitously, toward the Land of Israel. On the way, God gave the Jews the Torah at Mount Sinai, sealing our transition from a group of twelve disparate tribes into a nation, the first nation defined not by land or language, but by a covenant.

Ironically, for a holiday that celebrates Jews becoming a free people, one can easily feel like a slave getting ready for it. Like all religious Jewish homemakers, Nana had been strenuously cleaning house for weeks. Since anything with leavening (*chametz*) is forbidden during Pesach, Nana scoured counters, the inside of her oven, and the refrigerator shelves, and stowed away the *chametz* pots, pans, flatware and sets of dairy and meat dishes that she used during the rest of the year. On countertops and shelves antiseptic enough on which to perform surgery, Nana lined every surface with gleaming aluminum foil, giving her kitchen a futuristic, NASA-type look. These completely *chametz*-free surfaces accepted Nana's Passover cookware, dishes, cutlery, baking supplies, oils, and soup mixes. On Papa's modest income as a rabbi, Nana didn't have money for household help, so by the time we arrived for seder, Nana had earned her exhaustion.

"Oy, I've been verking so hard, you don't know," she greeted us. "*Iz shver tzu zayn a Yid*," she said, shaking her head. *It's hard to be a Jew.*

We nodded sympathetically, and like good therapists reflected back Nana's conclusion that she had worked very hard. Mom and her sister, Aunt Eleanor, helped by saying they couldn't wait to taste the chicken soup and the brisket, whose succulent aromas filled the kitchen.

Presiding at the table set with Nana's fine Passover china, Papa Cohen stood, his silver goblet filled to the brim with the Manischewitz wine. Like his father, grandfather, and countless ancestors through the centuries, Papa held the goblet cupped in his right hand as he recited the kiddush, the prayer sanctifying the holiday:

> *Blessed are You, HaShem our God, King of the universe, who has . . . sanctified us with His commandments. And You gave us, HaShem our God with love, festivals for gladness, festivals and times of our joy, the day of this Festival of Matzos, the time of our freedom . . . Blessed are You, HaShem, Who sanctifies Israel and the festival seasons.*

This was just so much mumbo jumbo to Papa Rosenfeld, who had a very different way of presiding over formal dinners in his own home. With guests seated around the table, Papa would stand at the head of the table holding aloft a crystal goblet with expensive, unkosher wine. Smiling mischievously, Papa would say, "Here's to those who wish me well, and all the rest can go to hell!"

I felt utterly scandalized by Papa Rosenfeld's toasts even as I was secretly thrilled by his brashness. But Papa Cohen's sincerity as he made the kiddush at the seder touched me. I could almost see the spirits of our ancestors in the room, watching, listening, and nodding with approval.

That fateful seder night, while reading about the Exodus from Egypt in the Hagadah, the battle of the soup bowls played out as usual. Like many traditional bubbies, Nana considered food a form of security, and her personal preparation and delivery of it a form of love. With her apron tied around her formal holiday dress, Nana hovered over us wielding a large stainless steel soup ladle, threatening to dole out seconds of her chicken soup even as we haplessly tried to stop her.

"No thank you, Nana," we'd say.

"Vy not?" she'd ask. It was a rhetorical question. "It's delicious!" We tried to shield the tops of the bowls with our hands but had to jerk them away as that second helping cascaded in. Refusing a second bowl was hurtful enough to Nana, but my sister, Sharon, refused even a first, small helping. Sharon wasn't a defiant sort. She just didn't like soup, not anybody's soup. Like a seasoned saleswoman, Nana pretended not to hear Sharon's "No." As my older sister helplessly watched Nana's full ladle steaming toward her like a culinary gunboat, she protested.

"Nana, you know I don't like soup!"

"Yes you do!" Nana persisted, though Sharon truly did not like soup. To this day, Sharon will not eat soup, not even mine, and trust me, my soups are also delicious.

"You von't get chopped liver if you don't eat my soup," Nana said, dangerously upping the ante. "And I verked so hard on the chopped liver! Do you want to see all the bowls I used to make it?" Nana waved her free hand over to the kitchen counter, where the used bowls sat as silent witnesses to Nana's testimony. Now, my sister loved Nana's chopped liver as much as she detested hot soup, and protested the unfairness of the deal.

"Mama, let Sharon have the chopped liver. Please." Mom eventually prevailed, freeing Sharon from the tyranny of unwelcome chicken soup. My sister was allowed to have her chopped liver and eat it, too.

Sitting through the recital of the tale of the Israelites' travails in Egypt was bondage enough for Papa Rosenfeld's atheist sensibility.

Watching Nana's attempts to force-feed my sister archetypal Jewish food was unendurable. As the argument over the soup heated up, Papa Rosenfeld could take no more. "Jesus Christ!" he muttered loudly.

Papa Cohen shot Papa Rosenfeld a withering look. Papa Cohen was a reserved and decorous man, but there are some things you just didn't say at a rabbi's home on seder night. "Jesus Christ" was one of them. Cece lightly placed a calming hand on Papa's knee and whispered something that subdued him for the rest of the evening. This was the last supper for Herbert and Cecelia Rosenfeld at Rabbi Bernard and Ethel Cohen's home.

I always knew that Nana and Papa Cohen's devotion to Judaism was real and deep. Their service was loyal and heartfelt. Yet, too often, Nana's obsessive worrying and Papa's borderline stern demeanor made it seem joyless, the stuff of duty and habit. That's why I also felt a little sad each year when we went to their house for seder. Nana and Papa wanted nothing more than to instill their love of Judaism in their grandchildren. But if, as Nana kept repeating, it was really so *shver tzu zayn a yid*, why would any of us bother?

I don't mean to be hard on poor Nana. Where she came from in Ukraine, it was indeed hard to be a Jew, frightening and dangerous. Why, where Nana grew up in Kiev, violence against Jews was a relentless tyranny. In just three years, from 1918 to 1921, a mind-numbing 1,300 pogroms killed tens of thousands of Jews across Ukraine, when Nana was a young teenager. Hundreds of Jewish villages were pillaged and left in ruins and a half a million Jews were left homeless. Life became unbearable for so many Jews, it's no wonder they were desperately scraping together every kopek they could to buy their way to safety across the ocean.

I understood why Nana, like thousands of other Jewish immigrants of her generation, endlessly repeated this meme in America.

But it was a deadly motto, one that undoubtedly sparked countless thousands of intermarriages.

Growing up, I constantly wondered: Could I possibly carve out a life that would blend the best of my grandparents' distinct and singular worlds? I wanted to live the kind of broadly intellectual, even cosmopolitan and fun life that Cece and Papa Rosenfeld lived. I wanted more *joie de vivre* than *oy de vivre.* Cece and Papa had traveled to Europe and planned to take me there, too. I was fascinated by their bookshelves, which featured titles by Graham Greene, Walt Whitman, William Shakespeare, Gunter Grass, and even Eldridge Cleaver. At Nana and Papa's house, I couldn't even read most of the titles of the books on the heavily laden shelves. They were mostly tall, thick volumes of the sacred works and commentary in Hebrew and Aramaic.

There was one very funny exception, a small paperback biography of Elizabeth Taylor. During Papa's tenure as a pulpit rabbi at a synagogue in Las Vegas, he had performed her wedding to Eddie Fisher, and hitched Eydie Gourmet and Steve Lawrence as well. Papa was named in that biography of La Liz, so the book made it into the Cohen library. But otherwise, their all-Jewish, all-the-time intellectual interests felt narrow to my teenaged self.

Cece and Papa were a hard act to follow, with Papa's jokes, their eclectic circle of friends, Cece's adoring patients, and their worldly outlook. But I wasn't willing to discard the Jewish values that Nana and Papa tried so hard to teach. I knew they included loyalty to tradition, honesty, kindness, honor, and a certain gravitas toward life. Frankly, each set of grandparents had something the other was missing. Every time I arrived at my Rosenfeld grandparents' home, my eyes instantly gravitated toward the front doorpost, where there was no mezuzah. Inside the house, there was no silver kiddush cup, even in a display case, no Jewish prayer book. Nothing said, "This is a Jewish home."

I wanted to have some of Nana and Papa's religious feeling, but without the stuffiness and certainly without the angst. Was there a way to fuse a life of eclectic interests (Communism not included) while also keeping kosher and staying loyal to my Jewish heritage? How I wished someone would model that kind of Judaism where I could see it.

Chapter 3

SEVEN CIRCLES

JULY 12, 1987

ROBIN SIGNALS TO MY PARENTS AND ME THAT she's about to open the doors to the hall where the wedding ceremony will take place. I begin trembling visibly. The nervousness I've tried to tamp down is now exploding in every cell of my body. My grip on my bouquet tightens mercilessly, and I am probably choking all the life out of these beautiful blooms, but I cannot help it. I'm a nervous wreck. I walk according to the slow, measured pace Robin has instructed toward my parents, who are waiting for me mid-aisle, and smile nervously at the two hundred and twenty-five guests who have risen from their seats in my honor. I can't see as clearly as usual since I didn't want to wear my glasses during the ceremony, but I can see that everyone stands when I enter the room. Quite a nice touch, I think.

But when I look ahead toward the chuppah, the wedding canopy, I feel a stab of disappointment. Jeff is facing the wrong direction! Instead of gazing in loving adoration at me in all my bridal beauty, he is facing the rabbi, his head bowed slightly and his body bobbing forward and backward almost imperceptibly. He is praying. Now he's missing the single moment when he should be staring at me, agog at my professionally applied bridal beauty!

Jeff is wearing a long white linen robe, or *kittel*, over his suit. The *kittel* signifies purity and it was purchased for the wedding. However, unlike my wedding dress, which is a single-use item, the *kittel* now becomes a significant garment in Jeff's life. He will wear it every Yom Kippur and Passover seder from now on. At the end of his life, he will be buried in it. When I climb the few steps of the riser and stand next to Jeff, he looks so handsome and sweet that I forgive him for praying instead of gazing at me when I made my entrance.

We have chosen a simple set-up for the chuppah, a canopy open on all sides. We are using Jeff's new prayer shawl, or *tallis,* tied with four poles, as the chuppah. Each pole is held by an honored guest. The chuppah's openness demonstrates our commitment to building a home that will be open to guests, just like the tent of Abraham and Sarah, our forebears.

I begin to make the seven circuits around Jeff, with my mother and mother-in-law on either side of me. Rabbi Lapin, who is performing our wedding and is also our new rabbi in the small congregation in Venice where we are starting our lives together, has explained to us that my walking around him seven times signified the private space I am creating around our relationship, sort of like the protected airspace of a sovereign country. Seven is a big number in Judaism that represents wholeness and completion. *Shabbos* is the seventh day of the week; there are seven notes in the musical scale; seven colors of the rainbow, and seven directions (including forward, back, and center). While no one would ever accuse me of being mystically inclined, I cannot help but find it striking how many notable "sevens" there are, signifying a unifying spiritual element in the physical world. In the merging of our two lives into an integrated whole, Jeff and I will also be considered complete.

At first, I had liked the idea of walking around Jeff seven times. It was an active, subtly dramatic way in which I inaugurated our wedding ceremony. But now I'm so nervous I'm not sure I still know how to count to seven. I look hopefully at Rabbi Lapin each time I circle back, like a kid asking from the back seat, "Are we there yet?" He nods at me encouragingly to keep going, perhaps seeing that I am so nervous I might collapse. Finally, I finish, slightly dizzy, and take my place again next to Jeff.

Jeff's dad, Bob, is teary-eyed. His only son, his little "Yossele," is getting married. Jeff's mom, Laura, simply looks happy. My mom is maintaining her "We'll see about all this" expression, and my dad looks as if he is hoping that his hearing aid won't begin to whistle inconveniently during the ceremony. Michael Medved, the cofounder of our congregation, stands just outside the chuppah, singing "Baruch Haba," a welcome song that affirms God's might and asks Him to bless the bride and groom. I am so pleased by Michael's presence and participation in our wedding. He and his wife, Diane, have already proven themselves kind and caring to us. We're so pleased to call them friends.

Rabbi Lapin recites the kiddush over the wine and another prayer over the consecration of marriage. Then, after a nod from Rabbi Lapin, Jeff places the slim gold wedding band on the forefinger of my right hand and says, "With this ring, you are consecrated to me according to the law of Moses and Israel." Uttering this line in front of witnesses, with the ring on my finger, seals the deal. We are married now, I think happily, beginning to calm down.

Orthodox weddings can be beautiful, but they are very legalistic. There is no exchanging of vows or poetry readings, no improvising at all. I had wondered why it had to be so dry, and Rabbi Lapin had told me, "Under the right circumstances, marriages that begin legally will end up romantically, but marriages that begin based on romance alone will end up legally."

I saw his point. It's easy to get swept off your feet, to fall in love for a variety of superficial reasons. Jeff and I both had painful memories from previous relationships earlier in our lives, relationships based on shallow attractions. If Rabbi Lapin was right, Jeff and I would have a beautiful, romantic, and solid marriage. God knows we spent enough time discussing, debating, and deliberating what our guiding principles would be, settling on where we could each compromise on levels of ritual observance, and drawing a line on where we could not. We were crafting a shared vision of the future, one that we knew would continue to evolve over time as life unfolded.

Rabbi Lapin reads the *ketubah* – the world's first prenuptial agreement and one that has been in continuous use for more than two thousand years. Ours has been designed, painted, and calligraphed in beautiful Hebrew by a woman named Deborah, a member of the PJC community. With a wink acknowledging a few of our favorite things, Deborah painted a tiny guitar for Jeff and a tiny chocolate chip cookie for me, camouflaged in the richly hued painting of the Venice beachfront, leading in the distance to Jerusalem. The text inside the artwork is in Aramaic, the legal language of the Talmud. There's no talk in the *ketubah* about promises to love, honor, obey, or take long walks on the beach, even the beachfront near our little synagogue. It is a declaration of a man's commitment to his wife, very pointedly his promise to provide his wife with food, clothing, and physical intimacy. Jeff would be obligated to pay a financial settlement in the case of divorce, and I have clear inheritance rights if I outlive him. Before the wedding, the *ketubah* was signed by two witnesses known to be *Shabbos*- and kosher-observant.

My stated obligations to Jeff in the *ketubah* are: nothing. Really, nothing. Jeff is making all the promises here. Rabbi Lapin reads the *ketubah* text quickly and clearly, followed by an abbreviated version in English. He then hands me the document. By accepting it willfully into my own hands I have signaled my agreement to the marriage. No Jewish woman can be forced into a marriage against her will. The *ketubah* is my personal possession, and I'm supposed to keep track of its whereabouts. But we already plan to have it framed to hang it in our living room. I shouldn't lose track of it there!

In one of our meetings before the wedding, I had asked Rabbi Lapin why the *ketubah* didn't obligate me to Jeff in any way at all, not even to cook a single meal or to provide him with physical intimacy or children. He answered in his typically politically incorrect manner.

"Women who are well treated by their husbands don't need to be told how to manage their marriages," he said. "For women, this is almost always intuitive. Only when a man doesn't do his job does a woman find it harder to do her job in a marriage." As usual, when Rabbi Lapin was speaking, I was alert for anything I was ready to disagree with. But I took a moment to digest this, and the concept, while a bit sweeping, still felt mostly true. Based on everything I had seen in the relationships around me, including my own parents' marriage, and those of my grandparents, most women genuinely are more inherently sensitive to the nuances of relationships than men.

I was still reorienting my worldview and self-image to accept the fact that Jewish Orthodoxy was not anti-woman. I had believed wholeheartedly that this was the case for most of my life, just by picking up the occasional dismissive comments from Reform and Conservative Jews about the Orthodox as hopelessly antiquated. Also, Papa Cohen's approach to life and to Judaism was so staid and solemn that I learned to think, "Wow, if he's this serious and only Conservative, I can't imagine how joyless the Orthodox must be!"

According to Jewish law, or halacha, roles for men and women were not the same, but that sounded less unfair when I realized that even among men, roles and duties differed depending on what ancestral lineage you had, such as being descended from the Kohanim versus from the tribe of Levi, or whether, like Papa Cohen, you were "just" Israel. The American ideal of equality, where separate could not mean equal, had no parallel according to Judaism: Each man and each woman was considered a precious and invaluable member of the larger Jewish community. Given that women have almost always lived in male-dominated societies, I have a newfound pride that the *ketubah* demonstrates such foresight and care about women's rights on every level.

Rabbi Lapin completes our wedding ceremony with the rest of the *sheva brachot*, seven blessings (there's that number again). My favorites are the last two:

> *Grant abundant joy to these loving friends, as You bestowed gladness upon Your created being in the Garden of Eden of old. Blessed are You, Lord, who gladdens the groom and bride.*
>
> *Blessed are You, Lord our G-d, King of the universe, who created joy and happiness, groom and bride, gladness, jubilation, cheer and delight, love, friendship, harmony, and fellowship . . . let there speedily be heard in the cities of Judah and in the streets of Jerusalem the sound of joy and the sound of happiness, the sound of a groom and the sound of a bride . . . Blessed are You, Lord, who gladdens the groom with the bride.*

Guests customarily sing along for the last verse of the last blessing, which infuses the room with a surging wave of joy and feeling of community. All that's left is for Jeff to stomp on a crystal wine glass, wrapped in a small velveteen sack. This custom is meant to inject a moment of solemnity into the occasion, reminding us that our joy can never be complete as long as Jerusalem's Third (and final) Temple has not been built. Ironically, you can almost feel the collective intake of breath as everyone watches the groom raise his leg and then stomp on the glass. Once everyone hears that satisfying *thud*, the tension is released, and hundreds of people spring up from their seats, singing, clapping, and shouting, "Mazal tov!" The musicians strike up the chords of "Od Yishama" once again.

Suddenly, we are rushed by relatives and friends. People are laughing and crying, singing and clapping. Oy, do Jews love weddings, probably more than they love Chinese food. Add Chinese food to the *hors d'oeuvres* at a Jewish wedding, and you've got one ecstatic people! Everyone wants to hug and kiss the bride and groom, even before we have had a chance to kiss each other in a private room immediately after the ceremony.

This is my Big Fat Orthodox Jewish Wedding, and it's an emotional event, even for guests who aren't relatives. Despite all our tragic history, despite rampant assimilation and intermarriage, another Jewish couple has decided to marry "according to the law of Moses and Israel." Another Jewish couple is thumbing their noses at our enemies, beating the odds against Jewish survival, voting for Jewish continuity, agreeing to keep the covenant. Another Jewish couple has looked into their hearts and toward heaven and declared, "Yes, God, we're still on Your team!"

Another "faithful house of Israel" has just been born. And that just makes almost everyone cry with happiness.

Chapter 4

"EVERY FAMILY IN THE WORLD..."

1973–1982

JEFF AND I ARE WHISKED AWAY AFTER THE CEREMONY, encircled by singing and dancing guests, as well as two musicians playing the clarinet and the flute. We have fifteen minutes alone to break our fast (Jeff's, anyway, since I blew mine this morning) and share our first kiss as husband and wife. Then we have to hustle outside for our "couple" pictures and the reception. But after our first kiss, we are too emotional to even eat. Since we're not eating, I attempt to put Jeff's wedding ring on his finger, but it's not going on without a fight. The literal heat of the moment has expanded Jeff's fingers, but God help me I'm determined to jam it on. Finally, he plunges his hand into a glass of ice water, and we laugh and laugh at the absurd way we are sharing our first moments as husband and wife. The ice water does the trick, and in a few minutes we each are wearing our wedding rings.

Double-ring ceremonies aren't done in Orthodox circles, because according to Jewish law, the point of a ring is that a bride, and only the bride, must receive financial consideration from the groom during the marriage ceremony in order for the marriage to be valid. But nothing prevents a man from wearing a ring, and Jeff was eager to wear his new symbol of his married status.

We eat a few bites of fruit and cake set out for us on a platter, agreeing that we had the best wedding ceremony in the history of matrimony. We are giddy with joy and excited to make our grand entrance into the ballroom, when the party pandemonium will break out in earsplitting earnest. We hear boisterous voices out in the hallway, the sounds of revelry that promise an exciting bash. Guests are undoubtedly snapping up the canapés, mini hot dogs and other *hors d'oeuvres* as they wait for the real dinner, which won't be served until after the first dance.

We are grateful to our parents for paying for this big bash, especially when our decision to embrace Torah tradition may still have seemed strange to them, if not regressive. We know very well how parents can often feel hurt or even repudiated by choices like ours. Hurting our parents is the last thing we want, but like almost every generation, we are forging our own way, confident that ours will be a more "enlightened" way than the path that our parents had forged. Isn't that so often the way as each generation comes of age?

One thing we are very determined about is to limit TV consumption not only for ourselves but for our kids. I look back in horror at the endless hours I squandered as a kid watching insipid soap operas, dumb sitcoms or forgettable Movies of the Week for years on end when billions of otherwise healthy brain cells probably committed suicide.

My media consumption had a darker side as well. I was a voracious reader from the beginning and gorged on news stories in the daily paper and news magazines. As a young child in the Age of Aquarius, I was too aware of the cultural upheavals of the 1960s for my own good, and my excessive media consumption taught me that the world I lived in was filled with endless trauma and self-destruction. I knew about the Kent State campus uprisings, fatal drug overdoses by teenagers and young adults, the traumatizing assassinations of Robert Kennedy and Martin Luther King. Violence loomed close to home when Charles Manson and his sick "family" committed the grisly Tate-La Bianca murders a few miles from where Cece and Papa lived, adding to my sense of a world gone dangerously mad. And the Vietnam War was no abstraction to us: my brother Allan would turn eighteen in September of 1970. Around the dining room table, I heard my parents and grandparents worry openly about his draft number. What would happen if he got sent to that faraway, bloody battleground? It was unimaginable.

We even ate dinner with the small kitchen TV set tuned into Walter Cronkite's newscast, passing the hamburgers and potatoes as America's anchorman reported the day's tally of dead, wounded, and missing in action in Southeast Asia in his authoritative, mournful tone. I had always wished we had more conversation among us, but Dad's severe hearing loss and Mom's reticence to share her feelings about most topics conspired to fill the airspace with talking media heads, not our own voices. It was a poor surrogate for family time.

"Don't trust anybody over thirty," became the mantra of college-aged kids, but it didn't seem to me such a great idea to trust the judgment of a generation so eager to tear down almost everything that was traditional and structured. Why did everything have to be overturned? Even as a little kid I knew that champions of this societal revolution were often stoned.

The world around me already felt very unstable when our private world was plunged into grief. On March 5, 1970, I arrived home at dusk after Hebrew School, alarmed to find my mom waiting for me on the front lawn. She was wearing a white wool coat and standing slightly bent over so I could not see her face. I panicked. She never waited for me outside like that. Something was disastrously wrong.

I ran out of the car and looked up at her tearful, pained face. She could barely utter the impossible words: "There's been a very bad accident, and Allan is . . . dead."

I burst into tears and held her tightly. Despite my shock and burying my face into her chest I saw from the corner of my eye Dad storming out the front door and around the front lawn with a pounding step, then circling back into the house, the screen door slamming.

Allan was dead. It was beyond shocking, a dizzying, sickening piece of news. I had seen him in his bed asleep that morning, since I often took a shortcut through his room to the kitchen. I knew he had planned to drive to Pacific Palisades to visit Cece and Papa, because it was Cece's birthday that day and Papa's birthday the next. Going along Mulholland Drive from the San Fernando Valley to the Westside, the car he was driving plunged off the road and into the steep canyon.

Allan had been the big brother I adored, my protector and defender. I ran to him for refuge when I had annoyed my older sister, Sharon, to the point I needed to get out of her way. He lifted me high so I could dunk the basketball in the hoop nailed to the garage, and he coached me on how to get the knight from Papa Rosenfeld during games of chess. While the rest of us were dark-haired, Allan was dark blonde, six foot one, and very handsome. His room was crowded with sports trophies from being a star of the high school basketball team, and certificates for academic achievements. He was slated to head off to San Diego State University in a few months.

Almost all our close family friends and relatives were packed inside our small house, everyone in shock. People stood and spoke quietly, crying. Mom sat at the end of the couch, sobbing, her best friend at her side. Huddled in the backyard were a knot of Allan's friends and Sharon and her friends. Nana and Papa Cohen, utterly stricken, stood close together in the dining room, where Papa so often presided over our Shabbos dinners. Cece and Papa Rosenfeld were sitting on the living room couch, and I eased myself into the small space between Papa and the arm of the couch. While my Cohen grandparents were the grandparents of faith, it was my apostate Papa who offered the only strangely comforting words I heard that day or for years after.

"Imagine," he said, "This happens to every family in the world." He shook his head sorrowfully.

Though I was only nine years old, somehow I understood Papa. I immediately understood that what he meant was that every family suffered loss at some time or other, that that loss was universal. If Papa was right, I realized that we could survive this bewildering anguish.

Wisely, my parents kept me away from the funeral. I sat with Cece and Papa at their home all day, no one really speaking, each of us indelibly heartbroken. Dad was least able to cope with the emotional tsunami that engulfed us. Over the weeks, months, and years to come, his grief turned to anger, sometimes explosive anger. It could erupt seemingly for no reason and it frightened me. When Dad got into a state, I stayed in my room, waiting for the storm to subside. My mother spent a lot of time trying to soothe Dad, sometimes waking him from nightmares. My insecurity skyrocketed. Allan had been alive in the morning and dead in the afternoon. What if something awful would next happen to Mom, Dad, or Sharon? I watched the clock obsessively when anyone was out, and panicked if anyone was unaccounted for ten minutes after they said they would be home.

Talking about feelings wasn't yet in vogue. People did not rush to therapy and support groups to help deal with grief, so we all suffered together, yet also painfully alone. Nobody had the language to provide support, no matter how much their hearts were with us. Mom was so consumed dealing with Dad that it probably didn't occur to her that I might have needed someone to talk to, too. Eventually, I heard Cece say that Dad needed professional help, but he refused to go. I think he may have thought it wasn't manly, and besides, touching those emotions and processing them was a place he couldn't go. While Dad had never been religious at all, after Allan died he refused to set foot in a synagogue unless it was for a special occasion, such as my bat mitzvah or similar celebrations.

At night in bed, I could not stop myself from replaying the vision of Allan's car going off Mulholland Drive. It was brutal. It was also tortuous for me to think of him in a coffin underground, so I conjured wild ideas: What if he had run away? Maybe he had been kidnapped? In either of those scenarios, he might come back to us one day. I knew these notions were preposterous, but they were better than thinking of the pure physical deterioration of my seventeen-year-old brother, so recently alive and vibrant, now dead.

We all struggled to forge ahead, but Allan's absence loomed over us. About a year later, I walked into Allan's room, which Mom was slowly turning into a den, and saw one of the most heartbreaking images of my life: Mom moving almost as if in slow motion, standing in the minuscule closet, packing up his clothes. My breath caught in my chest as I saw my beautiful strong mother, always supporting the emotional needs of my Dad, hold one of Allan's sweaters to her chest and bury her face in it. I hurried out of the room so she wouldn't see me cry or know that I could see her crying, too.

Dad's hearing deficit made it hard for him to get full-time work, which meant he was often home during the day. Though he was trained as a technician who provided eye exercises to children with optical muscle imbalances, he was also dependent on referrals from ophthalmologists, many of whom were unconvinced of the value of the treatments. Dad loved children and was very warm and sweet with them, but both children and their parents needed patience to communicate with him. His underemployment and sorrow combined to keep Dad both frustrated and depressed. Mom had recently gone back to college to finish her degree, planning to become a schoolteacher, and was out of the house a lot, and I found myself alone with Dad frequently when he would suddenly break down into an angry fit. I learned to calm myself down when he was in a tirade over something, often something trivial. When I saw he was on the edge but not yet over that edge, I mustered my courage and tried to soothe him, but I only had on-the-job training as a kid psychologist. I had to toughen up fast.

Allan's loss made the question of God and His existence more pressing to me over time. Who or What was God? Papa Rosenfeld's atheism meant I couldn't ask him. His own father died when Papa was about six, leaving his mother a poor widow with six children. According to Papa, the rabbi came over to their home and said that Papa's father's death was God's will.

"If that was God's will, I wasn't going to have anything the hell to do with Him," Papa said. He never looked back, forever disdaining the notion of a divine Being.

Yet I wasn't comfortable discussing this with Papa or Nana Cohen, either. I felt Nana would become too emotional to help, and Papa was always so busy studying, writing, or rushing off to one or another of his appointments that he seemed too busy for me to ask about God, though he probably would have welcomed my questions.

I suspected that God had to exist. The natural world was far too complicated not to have had a designer, but if God was real, did He really call the shots down here on Earth? Was Allan's death God's will? If so, how could that be? How could God take children from their parents, injecting lasting trauma and turmoil in so many lives?

I wanted answers.

It wasn't until I was already twenty-five, when I attended my first Torah class with Jeff, that I had any idea that Judaism believed in an immortal soul. Nana and Papa Cohen had never spoken about this idea, had never spoken of Allan's soul living on for eternity. Did they just assume that we all knew it, just as they had been taught and believed to be true? Whatever the reason for their silence on the issue, it was never discussed. When I first discovered that it was an essential tenet of Jewish belief that the soul lived on eternally, I began to look back at my prior Jewish education in wonderment and even resentment: how could a nice Jewish girl from Van Nuys who had never even been in a church know with certainty that Christians believed in an eternal soul but not that Jews believed in an eternal soul? When exactly did this fundamental idea get dropped from the Jewish syllabus? And why?

It had not been easy for me to even agree to attend Rabbi Lapin's classes at first, because he was Orthodox and that label carried a lot of baggage with me. I had assumed that if Nana and Papa were only Conservative Jews but seemed so deadly serious about everything, no way was I going to wade into the waters of Orthodoxy. Besides, my feminist ideas could not square with what I already "knew" were unequal roles for men and women within Orthodox circles. And just as I anticipated, I was rankled when I first heard Rabbi Lapin's criticisms of the exact type of Reform and Conservative education that I had had. Easy for you to criticize, I thought. At least they're egalitarian and modern, while you don't want anything to change! Yet grudgingly I began to agree with some of his pronouncements. If the modernizers of Jewish theology had dropped something so fundamental, so emotionally soothing, so life-affirming, something that my ancestors from time immemorial had known was true, they had committed educational malpractice.

Jeff and I knew that our life together would unfold in mysterious ways. We knew we would have to cope with challenges, pain, and loss because that's life. But in setting down roots within what Rabbi Lapin called a Torah-observant life, we also believed that we would have access to those spiritual truths that lay beyond our conception, certainly beyond anything we had been introduced to before. And we believed, hoped, and prayed that these truths, this wisdom, would help us build a strong marriage and family life, and guide us whenever we faced a rocky, uncharted path.

Adjusting to some of the new ideas that Rabbi Lapin was introducing, I still could not imagine why Allan had died, but I began to take some comfort that those I had already lost, not only Allan but Nana and Papa, and Cece and Papa, still lived on in what Rabbi Lapin called "the World of Truth."

Chapter 5

JOURNEYS NEAR AND FAR

1973–1982

I CARRIED MY BROTHER'S MEMORY IN my heart every day, but my childhood did not remain bleak; I had friends, I had an optimistic nature, and my parents even enrolled me in drama classes on weekends because I wanted to become an actress. (I had been born in a hospital in Hollywood, so maybe that had a subtle influence.) I was also grateful that Mom and Dad enjoyed a healthy social life, going out with other couples every Saturday night. As Cece had predicted, I spent a lot of my free time reading and writing and dreaming about becoming a writer.

My heroine was Erma Bombeck, and I snapped open the newspaper twice a week in eager anticipation of reading her latest hilarious column about life as a suburban wife and mother. She was wickedly funny and ironic, yet never mean-spirited. For Mother's Day, I bought my mom Erma's latest book, though I read it before Mom had a chance to. When I grew up, I wanted to be like

Erma, sharing the gift of laughter with my imagined massive reading audience.

I was sure that laughter was healing. Mom and I watched lots of comedy shows on TV in the evenings, laughing sometimes till tears rolled down our cheeks at the sidesplitting antics on *The Carol Burnett Show,* the brilliant comic timing and dialogue on *The Odd Couple* and *All in the Family.* It was wonderful to sit with my mom and laugh with her, wonderful to see that she had a respite from the pain that could never be far from her consciousness.

My blessings mounted. The summer I turned twelve, Cece took me to Europe for five amazing weeks. She and Papa had taken Allan and Sharon to Europe, each when they were twelve years old, but by the time my turn came Papa had been severely weakened by a stroke and was housebound. Family vacations with Mom and Dad were generally to San Diego for a few days each summer, so I was excited at the thought of the first-class private tour that Cece was planning for us. Europe!

Cece and I stayed at the finest hotels in London, Paris, Venice, Amsterdam, Rome and Zurich. My eyes bulged with awe and delight watching the changing of the guard at Buckingham Palace, and I was utterly enthralled by the grandeur of the Eiffel Tower, the masterpieces in the Louvre, fascinated by the antiquity of Rome's Coliseum, and captivated by the picture-book perfection of the Swiss Alps.

We drove deep into the verdant British countryside to visit the homeopath who had trained Cece. The sweeping branches of the old-growth trees made canopies of shade over the road, and the open countryside seemed to go on forever. Outside of movies, I had never seen such natural beauty or so much open land in my life. It was magical.

When I began to tire of homeopathic shoptalk, Sarah, our private guide, took me for a drive in her little European sports car on the quiet roads. Sarah was in her early twenties, pretty and bubbly. I thought she was absolutely fabulous. I knew a lot of the British pop songs she played on the radio, and we sang together at the top of our lungs, laughing with joy. As only a paid guide would have had the patience for, Sarah also indulged me as I recited the names of all the British kings and queens going back to William the Conqueror in 1066, a list I was memorizing at night for fun.

At home we had a framed picture of Allan when he had stood in St. Mark's Square in Venice, surrounded by pigeons, during his trip to Europe. When Cece and I arrived in that same open space, I couldn't stop thinking that Allan had stood there as well, perhaps in the very spot where Cece took my picture. As awed as I had been by the elegant Grosvenor House in London, I was even more daunted by the marble opulence of the Hotel Danieli, and gobsmacked when we arrived in Rome. I craned my neck to try to take in the stunning beauty and vastness of Michelangelo's ceiling in the Sistine Chapel. I was left speechless and with a sore neck. One afternoon as we were walking back to the Danieli, a young and very handsome man approached and began talking to us in rapid Italian. When he realized we were American, he punted to broken English and begged Cece to let me go out with him. She protested that I was only twelve, yet this seemed not to be a deterrent. I was both thrilled and scared. Things like this never happened to me back in boring old Van Nuys!

In fact, being the object of a romantic pursuit was as foreign to me as being served steak *tartare en flambé* under a shining chafing dish in Zurich or eating Yorkshire pudding in London. The boy on whom I had wasted my first crush earlier that year, Stuart, had rejected me utterly and consistently, though I was not discouraged and continued to hitch rides to Hebrew School on Wednesdays, where I could gaze at him furtively during class breaks. He responded to my ill-concealed ardor by sneering, "Hey, fatty!"

whenever he saw me in the hallway. Pained yet still on a mission, I continued this midweek practice of self-immolation until one day, one final "Hey fatty!" greeting finally knocked some sense into me. My stalking was not having the desired effect! Stuart would never find me worthy of his affections and would almost certainly never find me thin enough.

My five-minute near-romance in Venice was a sorely needed boost to my nascent feminine ego. It also reassured me that handsome men didn't mind an extra few pounds on a girl. Cece and I laughed about this episode over and over again as the weeks flew by. We sailed down the Rhine River, tromped through castles in France, and awoke one morning to the sound of a little goat bleating on a hillside in Gruyère, Switzerland, where I pretended to like the smelly cheeses we tasted in a local factory. It was the trip of a lifetime, and it did exactly what Cece and Papa had intended by expanding my world through travel.

While Cece and Papa made sure I saw Europe, Nana and Papa made sure I saw Israel. It was a grand gift right after my bat mitzvah when they took Mom and me to the Holy Land the following summer. I was startlingly moved when we arrived at the Western Wall in Jerusalem, often referred to as the "Wailing Wall" because of the heartfelt prayers recited against its smooth, ancient stones. Even though it is only the remaining outer wall of the huge complex that encompassed the courtyard of the Second Temple, destroyed in the year 70 CE, both Jews and non-Jews have prayed here since the time of Abraham. I, too, wedged a folded scrap of paper with a handwritten prayer into the crevices of the huge stones, which somehow endlessly absorb these entreaties from deep in the heart.

In Europe, I had been wowed by the sprawling castles and immense churches that were hundreds of years old. But in Israel, "vintage" was measured not in hundreds of years but in thousands. Our tour of the excavated fortress at Masada, built on a cliff overlooking the Dead Sea, shocked me. Around two thousand years ago, Jews had built a community there, complete with houses and a ritual bath, while fleeing from the Romans. I simply could not begin to fathom what it was like to live in antiquity, nor to have to run for my life to a remote mountaintop because I was hated so much for being Jewish. For Nana and Papa, who left their own families behind in Europe, leaving also the continent's interminable anti-Semitism, this idea was no abstraction. Papa's parents, Yoel Hersh and Raisel, his brother Kalman, as well as many, many cousins, had all been murdered by the Germans. On the Israel trip, where our accommodations were closer to Spartan than splendorous, we also met some of Nana and Papa's cousins who had fled east during the Nazi scourge. I was so touched by their instant affection for us, their warmth, and their insistent asking us, "When are you moving here?"

I realized on this trip that while Europe had been astonishing and broadening, Israel touched me personally: everywhere we went, whether an amphitheater at Caesarea, the cisterns built by King David, the remains of a mosaic tile floor of a synagogue, or excavations of homes in the Old City of Jerusalem, I was reminded that I, Judy Rosenfeld, was a link in a very long and unbroken chain of Jewish history.

After that trip, I decided to try to get some answers about God and made an appointment to speak to our rabbi at the synagogue. I had logged a lot of time in Hebrew school, listened to the rabbi's Friday night sermons, and had just come from the Holy Land. I had been alert for any new information about God, but my perception of Him was still remote, fuzzy and childish. My Jewish education had taught me a little conversational Hebrew, a little bit about the holidays, and to love and feel proud of the State of Israel. But God barely rated even a cameo appearance in any discussions.

In the rabbi's book-lined study, I asked him to explain what God was all about. I sat forward in eager anticipation of his answer.

He held his chin in his hand and looked deep in thought for what seemed like a very long time. When he finally spoke, he said, "When I see a beautiful sunset, or hear beautiful music, I see and feel God."

Okay, I'm with you so far. Keep going, I thought.

He spoke further about occasions where he sensed God's presence, explaining it more as a feeling or sensation that came over him at various times. He and his wife had lost a child to Tay-Sachs disease, a genetic illness that was not uncommon among Ashkenazi Jews before the days of genetic screening tests; so he had known suffering. However, he did not say that God was the architect of all things in our lives, painful or otherwise. Of course, he knew about our family's loss, but he did not say that his child's life, or Allan's life, short as each had been, had a purpose or spiritual value. He was a kind man, generous with his time, and he took my question seriously. Still, I left confused and a little disappointed. I had hoped that God was more than just an emotion.

While my formal Jewish education remained scanty, I clung to my social involvement at the synagogue. I went on every activity with the youth program, and when I outgrew that, I got a job as the assistant to the youth director. In high school, I became a teacher's aide in the Hebrew School, happy that my synagogue was my home away from home. I enjoyed the feeling of *mishpacha*, of family, around the shul. My jobs also kept me away from home and the loneliness that hovered in the air.

As a teenager, I tasted occasional moments of spiritual uplift, moments that touched me and left me craving more. In ninth grade, I participated in a program called *Havurat No'ar* ("Youth Friendship Circle" or "Youth Fraternity"). At the end of each unit of study, we went for a weekend retreat in Malibu.

We spent these weekends at the appropriately named Camp Hilltop, high on a coastal ridge in Malibu. I was scared riding on the bus up the slender and windy road; after losing Allan I was anxious on any such high or windy side road. Our Shabbos morning services were held outdoors on a bluff overlooking the Pacific Ocean. I loved to sing aloud and pray in unison with friends, the wind blowing powerfully from the ocean, the sun glinting from the waves. I felt my spirit soar, and it brought me to tears.

This retreat was an innovative program that opened my eyes to modern Zionist history, learning about Jews in the Diaspora in modern times, and the relationship between modern anti-Semitism and the founding of the State of Israel. I was startled when the teachers asked us to consider the question: Are you primarily a Jewish American or an American Jew? The question went to the heart of our identities, to what made Jews unique as a people, and I realized that Nana and Papa Cohen would instantly answer "Jewish Americans" and Cece and Papa would answer "American Jews."

Throughout my teen years, I often asked myself this question, sometimes hearing the echoes of my cousins in Israel who asked us, "When are you moving here? When are you coming home?"

I began to understand and sympathize much more with Nana's worries and Papa's somberness when we learned about the Holocaust. We watched documentaries that made my stomach grip in horror, read Elie Weisel's novel *Night*, listened to testimony from survivors whose tattoos on their arms could only hint at the psychological scarring inside, watched a gripping play about a heroic Danish couple who risked their lives to save Jews, and participated in a disturbing group activity that was meant to teach us the dangers of groupthink.

The program succeeded in deepening my bond with my Jewish identity and history, though it taught little of religious practice. One weekend they brought up rabbis from the Chabad-Lubavitch movement. The rabbis' long beards, black coats, affinity for song and dance, and eagerness to wrap tefillin on the arms of the boys made them seem cute and quaint, although not religiously compelling.

I befriended one boy in the program, Steven, who stood out among the hundred and fifty or so of us because he had become Orthodox on his own. He wore a kippah on his head and tzitzit, whose fringes hung down from the four-cornered garment he wore under his shirt. I was drawn to Steven's soft-spoken intelligence, and we spent a lot of time together talking.

"I don't see any other way of life that makes sense to me," Steven explained about his decision one afternoon outside the dining hall. "I believe the Torah is true, and if it is true, we are obligated to follow it. The mitzvot add a lot of meaning to my life." I was amazed that Steven's parents had agreed to his request to send him to a religious high school in Israel. I had huge respect for the way Steven had dived deeply into Jewish observance and his independence in staking his own claim to Jewish spirituality in a way that far transcended what had been offered to him.

While everything he said to me made sense, I realized I lacked his spiritual thirst–and his spiritual depth. Nor was I bold or independent enough to venture into such uncharted territory as he had. Besides, from whom would I learn the ways of Orthodoxy? Papa and Nana Cohen's approach to their Judaism was so laden with a sense of duty that I could not imagine becoming as religious as they were.

My Jewish identity remained emotionally strong, but I never became ritually observant. After I was accepted to UCLA I was excited about moving into a Jewish co-ed co-op called the Westwood Bayit (Hebrew for house). The kitchen was kosher, with separate dishes and cookware for milk and meat, but having male and female college students living under one dilapidated roof was less than kosher. I wanted to bring one of my parents to check it out, but when I suggested the following Sunday, a house resident named Elliot nixed the idea.

"This Sunday's not good. We're having a *farbrengen* that day, and it might get a little wild," he told me. He explained that *farbrengen* was Yiddish for a "get-together" and one of the rabbis from the Chabad house from around the corner would be there. How wild could a party be when the guest of honor was one of those black-frocked, bearded, singing rabbis? I was banking on my parents letting me live at the Bayit and assumed Elliot was exaggerating the risk. I ignored his advice and Dad and I drove into Westwood the following Sunday.

I realized my mistake when Dad and I were getting out of the car about a block from the house. Even from that distance, I could hear the very loud singing of a drunken nature, revelers in full throttle. Dad could not hear it but he would once we got up the stairs. Elliot rushed over to me at the entrance. "I told you today wasn't good!" he said, as I heard something crash to the floor, followed by boisterous laughter. I was speechless. Wasn't drunkenness for goyim? That's what Nana always said.

Appalled, I sat next to Dad at the edge of the combination living room-dining room. I dared not even look at my father. Many of the twenty or so "Bayit'niks" in attendance were lavishly lubricated. Tequila and Scotch bottles littered the table, the furniture all looked as if it was rejected from a Salvation Army depot, and a chair was overturned. In previous years the Bayit had housed a fraternity, and the house was clearly in desperate need of an extreme makeover. The students ate, drank, and sang, following the lead of the rabbi who sang in Hebrew and Yiddish. Among the sparse decor was a small wall hanging of the Hebrew alphabet, and the rabbi began in a singsong melody to teach the letters as if we were kindergarteners. "ALEPH!" he bellowed, and the Bayitniks echoed, "ALEPH!"

"BET!" he shouted, aiming a long wooden pointer toward the letter but instead whacking an already tipsy-looking lampshade to the floor. Elliot looked at me in sympathy as the crowd laughed uproariously. I was sunk. My parents would never let me live in this atmosphere of freewheeling riot! Images of driving my old, beat-up, unreliable Datsun from Van Nuys and over the 405 freeway every day to get to school filled me with gloom. Defeated, I wanted to leave right away. Prolonging this visit would just rub kosher salt in the wound.

But Dad, who often said things that were wildly unexpected, turned to me and said, "This looks like a nice group of people. Reminds me of my days in Zeta Beta Tau." I just smiled at Dad, trying to hide my disbelief that he would still manage to judge this collection of students favorably, despite the circumstances. "We don't need to tell Mom about this part," he said, winking. Thankfully, neither of us was tempted to share any details with Mom, who, had she only known, would never have allowed me to set foot in the place again.

I lived in the Bayit for two years, where most of my housemates were usually sober and I rejoiced in new friendships and the camaraderie of living in a close-knit community of Jewish students. Many were activists with Jewish campus causes, with plenty of arguments among house members about political issues having to do with Israel. I stayed out of the fray, but in classic Jewish tradition, the fights were vehement, including some choice Yiddish invective and the occasional piece of already "distressed" furniture overturned in anger.

We cleaned house on Fridays and held *Shabbos* services in our living room, singing traditional Hebrew songs at the dinner table, which shook with each pounding of our collective hands. I tried to make my mark on the campus Jewish community by writing my first article for the Jewish student newspaper at UCLA and was proud to live in our tumbledown yet beloved hippyish house.

The next summer I nabbed a summer internship with a Jewish student press service in New York, a minor miracle given my almost nonexistent journalism portfolio. I was assigned to write a few stories that related to the new, burgeoning phenomenon of secular Jews becoming Orthodox. This was known as the Baal Teshuva (returnees to Judaism) movement, one that had allowed both Rabbi Noah Weinberg and Rabbi Daniel Lapin to tap into the communities they cultivated. I dressed in long sleeves and a knee-length skirt before getting on a non-air-conditioned D train into Williamsburg to interview one such family, thinking, *You have got to be religious to dress like this in July in Brooklyn.*

In my first assignment, I interviewed Naomi, a young mother who had grown up secular but had chosen to live by strict Jewish tradition with her husband. Hair covered by a scarf, dressed in a long skirt and long sleeves, Naomi was interrupted frequently by her three young children, asking for juice, snacks or stories, or simply needing a bit of taming as they bounced as high as the laws of gravity would allow on the well-worn, sturdy brown couches.

"My husband and I were both increasingly disillusioned with where society was going," Naomi explained as I scribbled my notes. "I also felt that I didn't want to follow the expected path of focusing on career first and family second. We began looking in our own backyard, in Judaism, and liked what we learned." The art in her home included a photograph of Jerusalem on an east-facing wall and photos of bearded, somber-looking rabbis. Large bookcases were filled to bursting with volumes of Talmud, prayer books, and commentary on Jewish sacred writings.

I listened to Naomi as I had listened to my friend Steve, with respectful interest and admiration, but from a distance, with journalistic reserve. I liked to feel that I was honoring Nana and Papa Cohen's legacy by pursuing Jewish journalism, but Cece and Papa Rosenfeld had also left a legacy, which was that the world was too broad to be limited by too much religious doctrine.

I put my new journalism experience to good use right away.

After that summer I transferred to UC Berkeley, where one of my good friends, a former Bayit'nik who had also transferred up north, was the new editor of the Jewish student paper on campus. Ben and I had taken several of the same English classes together at UCLA and sometimes read Shakespeare to each other aloud in the Bayit's dining room. I marched into his tiny office in the student union building and said, "Hi, I'm your new assistant editor. Give me a job."

"Welcome aboard!" he said, smiling broadly. I threw myself into my work at the newspaper, finding it infinitely more interesting than most of my classes, other than English Literature. I happily devoted hours and hours each week to writing, soliciting and editing articles, and selling advertising. I helped design and lay out the pages, and developed an eagle eye for setting even the narrowest line of type evenly to correct a line that had a mistake. I simply loved every second of the painstaking work. The whole experience for me was invigorating. Ben and I drove into an industrial area of San Francisco to get our five thousand copies of the newspaper, and I took a deep inhale of the smell of fresh ink, the smell of creativity, I thought. Ben and I were ecstatic when we saw "our baby," grinning with pride of ownership–or at least of midwifery. Having loaded our papers in the car, our fingers already getting blackened from the ink, we gleefully delivered them all over the Bay Area. I could have done this sort of work every day for the rest of my life.

Papa Cohen was also a writer, and very proud of my status as a student editor. One Friday night when I was home for a visit, I went with Mom and Papa to synagogue. This was during the holiday of Sukkot, and after services we were all enjoying refreshments outside in the sukkah booth. I was in the middle of a conversation with somebody when I felt a hand on my back suddenly pushing me forward, somewhat aggressively. It was Papa.

"This is my granddaughter!" he said, introducing me to a friend. "She is the editor of the Jewish paper at Berkeley!" I was happy to be a source of pride to Papa, providing some real *Yiddishe nachas* (joy and satisfaction, Jewish-style). In fact, at this point I was the only one of Papa's four grandchildren who felt enthusiasm for living Jewishly. It made me feel even more responsible to make my life as a Jew count for something.

Chapter 6

BACK IN THE USSR

SUMMER 1982

BEFORE LONG I GOT A CHANCE TO AFFIRM what my Jewish identity and family meant to me. Right after I graduated college, I went to the Soviet Union with my mother and her sister, my Aunt Eleanor. We went to visit Nana's sister, my Aunt Rosa, and her family in Kiev, fulfilling a promise that our family had made to Nana before she died.

Nana had courageously left Russia alone at the age of sixteen to join her father in San Francisco. Her mother and sister chose to stay behind. Nana never dreamed that it would be more than a half-century–fifty-two years!–until she saw Rosa again. Throughout my childhood, Nana had been eaten up with anxiety over her sister's fate. They had exchanged letters regularly from Nana's departure in 1922 until the reign of the murderous Josef Stalin. That's when Rosa's letters from Kiev abruptly ceased. Nana had no idea if her letters ever arrived or even if they might put Rosa in danger.

When the letters stopped in the 1950s, Nana Cohen began her own long, valiant campaign to locate and reunite with her sister. For years, her efforts all led to dead ends. Undaunted, Nana applied to every Russian connection she had to discover Rosa's whereabouts, and in the mid-1960s my grandmother's efforts paid off. She found an intermediary in Russia who confirmed that Rosa, her husband, and their two children were alive and well. This third party helped smuggle letters between the sisters for years until they were allowed to correspond more freely in the 1970s. Sometimes more than a month would elapse between the time a letter was written and when it was received. To Nana, every letter received from Rosa was a cause for joy.

"Look! Liebe! Judy! I got a letter from Rosa today!" Nana would wave the white envelope so we could see the evidence, the handwriting on the outside a curious blend of English letters with a Cyrillic accent. The writing paper itself was almost as thin as onion skin. We all sat down as Nana excitedly translated it for us from Russian. (The sisters didn't dare write in Yiddish.)

"Vuhn day I'm going to see my *shvester* again," Nana would vow. And in 1974, she booked her flight to Moscow, and another flight from Moscow to Kiev, for the long-anticipated reunion. Nana was then sixty-nine and her health was no longer robust. At the airport, her gait was slow but her spirit was soaring. Papa, Mom, Aunt Eleanor and I hugged and kissed her goodbye, waving happily as she disappeared onto the Jetway, carrying her signature oversized "pocketbook," as she always called her purse.

We were all proud of Nana and excited for her, too. It took grit and courage to take this trip at her age. Just as she had left Russia alone fifty-two years earlier, now she was journeying back in the twilight of her life, alone again, to see her beloved sister. Nana and Rosa spent two weeks nestled together on the sofa in Rosa's tiny apartment, sharing sisterly confidences, memories, successes, heartbreaks, and secrets. Nana returned home bursting with stories about her *shvester* Rosa, her husband, their two children, Nella and Victor, and Victor's two children.

"Vee sat and cried and cried," Nana reported, and it was only too easy to visualize their steady cascade of tears–tears of joy at this second chance for togetherness; tears of sorrow over the lost opportunities for togetherness in years past, and for the troubles that each had suffered.

I noticed that all the pictures Nana took of the family were inside Rosa's apartment, with everyone crowding together to squeeze in, seated on the couch and crowding behind it or leaning in to the camera's lens at the dining room table. I asked about why all the photos were taken inside.

"Vhut do you think? Jews can't afford to call attention to themselves by taking pictures in public over there. They've got enough trouble," Nana explained.

I thought about Nana a lot while she was over in the Soviet Union. Picturing her in an environment with such a stark history of oppression of Jews, I reconsidered her overzealous demonstrations of love for her family. Yes, she could be pushy about what we ate, and how much. As if we could possibly forget, she reminded us, "You don't know how much I vorry about all of you," shaking her head like a comically overdramatized character in a play. As my Jewish identity began to mean more to me, I also regretted her well-worn, ruinous line, "*Iz shver tzu zayn a Yid.*" It's hard to be a Jew.

With dawning understanding, I realized that Nana's anxiety had not appeared in a vacuum. While she had left the cold thuggery of Russia, the fear of that cold thuggery had never left her. Even in America, where she and Papa lived a good and safe life, Nana could never completely shake the fear that underneath the surface of most non-Jews were anti-Semites who might want to do her or her family harm.

Nana promised Rosa that she would return. Even when Nana was diagnosed with cancer a year and a half later, she continued to visualize this second reunion with Rosa and battled her illness with determination and grace. Ironically, now that she was so ill and had something serious to worry about, she stopped talking about her worries. Instead, she spoke with optimism about her two goals: "I need to be better for our vedding anniversary party, and to go back and see Rosa again," she'd say. In fact, Mom and Aunt Eleanor were planning a gala fiftieth-anniversary party for Nana and Papa, with one hundred and fifty guests expected. At the anniversary party, Nana was weak and pale, but still beautiful in her black and gold, beaded floor-length gown. We all knew she would never return to Kiev.

"Promise me you'll go back and see Rosa, Nella, and Victor," Nana said to Papa, Mom, and Aunt Eleanor. "You've got to promise! They're our *family*." They promised.

Several months after the party, Nana knew her time had come. Mom was at her bedside at the hospital late at night. Nana could barely speak, but she turned to Mom and whispered, "Go see who's out in the hallway."

Mom went out to look. "There's nobody here but the nurses, Mama." It was already halfway to dawn. Nana closed her eyes and nodded. A few minutes later she said, "My mother is vatching over me." Nana's mother had passed away in Russia nearly thirty years earlier. My grandmother slowly turned her head to Mom and told her to stand up. Mom stood. In a soft voice, Nana called her name and said, "Bless you." Those were her last words.

Mom, Aunt Eleanor, and Papa fulfilled their promise and arrived in Kiev two years later, in 1979, hefting several suitcases filled with coveted American jeans, shirts, slacks, shoes, and children's clothing that our cousins had wanted very much. Mom and Aunt Eleanor had taken Russian lessons and had sat together at our dining room table, practicing expressions such as *Kak dela*? (How are you?), *Dobroe utro*! (Good morning!), and *Skol'ko eto stoit?* (How much is this?). They boned up on their spoken Yiddish, which they already understood well, so they could speak with Aunt Rosa. Meanwhile, Rosa's daughter, Nella, diligently studied English to prepare for the visit and interpret between Rosa and the rest of the family.

Aunt Rosa and their cousins showered Mom and Aunt Eleanor with love, plied them with bountiful, delicious Russian food, and simply could not do enough to demonstrate their happiness at the visit. Mom and Aunt Eleanor were overwhelmed by the experience, kept up a correspondence with Nella afterward, and even planned a second trip for the summer of 1982. Nobody asked me if I wanted to go, but a trip to the Soviet Union to meet my family sounded like a once-in-a-lifetime opportunity, and I spoke up. At eighty-two, Papa was not up to a second long journey, and he very generously offered to pay for my trip as a college graduation gift. Now it was my turn to learn to practice saying *Dobroe utro*! I had taken Yiddish at Berkeley for pure enjoyment, but now I was happily surprised that it would actually have a practical use when speaking with my great-aunt.

Relations between the Soviet Union and the US were abysmal that summer. President Reagan had been calling the Soviet Union "the evil empire" for some time, and the feeling was mutual. The moment we deplaned in Kiev, customs agents swooped down on us. Without asking our names they yanked Aunt Eleanor away from us and hustled Mom and me into a cavernous, bare room. We were alone with a stone-faced woman who had the warmth of a spray of mustard gas. She ordered us to open our suitcases and recklessly pawed through every stitch of clothing we had, almost hurling things angrily around on the table.

"How long veel you leeve in da Soviet Union?" she barked, not looking up from her scrutiny of our clothing, shoes, toiletries, and books. I had never before met anyone so filled with the vodka of human enmity. Sour Svetlana seemed like a parody of a character from a movie. But she was all too real.

I was frightened. "We are only here for a two-week visit," I said, hoping she did not assume I wanted to *leeve in da Soviet Union,* a thought that turned my blood to ice. I wished I had the courage to say *Ostav'te menja v pokoe!* (Leave me alone!), but that could have been suicidal. We had been in the country for less than twenty minutes when I began to think that the "evil empire" phrase was rather apt. We were forced to repeat the same answers to the same questions Sour Svetlana kept asking: Why had we come? Did we have relatives here? Where did they live? Had we brought gifts? Obviously she already knew the answers to all these questions, because we had had to explain the purpose of our trip on our visa applications. We had no choice but to admit the children's clothes were gifts, but we claimed that everything else, including men's clothing, was ours, though it was a ludicrous amount of clothing for two people on a two-week trip. The Soviets saw no earthly reason for any consumer goods to be brought in from outside the country, so rich in natural resources, yet essential consumer goods and even food staples were rationed.

"Take your things," she commanded after finishing her man-handling of the contents of one suitcase, strewn across a long table. We hardly had time to stuff it all back in as she ordered us impatiently to open the next suitcase. Eight green-uniformed and equally stone-faced lemmings marched in and out of the room as Sour Svetlana handed them various belongings of ours, including jewelry, our camera, and cash. They disappeared with our things, and I was sure we'd never see them again.

"Do you know da rules of da Soviet Union?" she asked, turning shirts inside out, unfurling lipstick tubes, and thumbing through books. Her careless handling of our possessions made it clear this inspection was not so much an effort to find contraband as it was to intimidate us. It worked.

"Yes!" I said, frightened into saying something that stupid. The only rule I understood now was not to argue with this loathsome individual. She was desperately in need of a Dale Carnegie seminar, and I was wobbly with fear. Where had they taken Aunt Eleanor? When would this ordeal be over? This hardly seemed the way to encourage more tourism, and if this was how they greeted other foreign visitors, I imagined the line to wait to see Lenin's tomb would be rather short.

To my surprise, the green-uniformed apparatchiks, walking in an almost comical mechanized style, marched back with our jewelry, cash, and camera and returned them to Sour Svetlana. "You are coming into the Soviet Union with these things and you vill leave with them, *or you vill be punished,"* she threatened, lengthening out each syllable of the last phrase. When she riffled through the last of our things, she suddenly said to us, "Go!" Our hearts pounding, we skedaddled, following one of the apparatchiks who took us to a public waiting area. We looked for Aunt Eleanor outside the airport, and heaved a sigh of relief when we heard her call eagerly, "Libby! Judy! Victor and Nella are here!"

Our cousins, Nana's niece and nephew, were waiting for us outside, bearing a huge bouquet of flowers and beaming. I fell into Nella's arms and burst into tears. I was exhausted after our twenty-six-hour journey, rattled by our encounter with the Soviet welcome committee, and unbelievably grateful for this moment. Finally, I was actually with my family members, whom I had known only through small Polaroid photos and through letters. We were together at last! We were taken to Rosa's apartment in a car driven by someone from Intourist, the Soviet Union's official state travel agency that controlled all visitor access to all Soviet citizens. Victor and Nella followed in a taxi.

Looking out the window, I saw the famous beauty of Kiev's bountiful parks and large forest-like swathes of greenery. The natural splendor belied Kiev's murderous history against my ancestors.

(This wasn't only at the hands of the Russians. On this trip, we planned to visit the memorial site at Babi Yar, where in 1941 the Nazis perpetrated the largest single massacre of Jews during the Holocaust–nearly 34,000 within two days.) When we arrived in my family's neighborhood, I was equally shocked by the endless gray of the long, rectangular apartment buildings, one after another, uniformly dreary and featureless. I had read some Kafka in college. Now I knew where he got the inspiration. Clearly, the architect must have been directed on pain of death to design the buildings for maximum depressive effect.

When Aunt Rosa opened the door, smiling from ear to ear, her plump grandmotherly arms wide open to envelop us in a tight embrace, I felt a shock of emotion. She looked so much like Nana! She was just a little shorter and a little rounder, and I felt Nana's presence indisputably hovering over us. Aunt Rosa and I held one another tight, both of us crying. I had not expected the moment to be so powerful, and for the first time I could begin to feel the impact of how different my fate had been compared to that of Rosa and her children and grandchildren. Nana had risked a journey to America, not knowing what awaited her. This risk allowed me to enjoy a freedom my aunt and cousins had never known. I could wear a Star of David necklace in public, attend rallies in support of refuseniks like Natan Sharansky, whose arrest on charges of treason in 1977 for supporting the "Zionist state" and for his request to emigrate to Israel made him an international hero. I was free to study Hebrew in public schools and to sing "Am Yisrael Chai!" in the streets on Israel Independence Day. My family in Kiev had to whisper–even in their drab little apartments–about anything that had the word "Jew" or "Jewish" associated with it.

Rosa's apartment felt tinier in person than it had appeared in pictures. The appliances were weirdly diminutive and outdated, the furnishings shabby, certainly by Western standards. When they invited two other couples to dine with us one night, Rosa's dining room table filled the living room to standing-room-only status with only a dozen people. The kitchen could hold three people at most, the bathroom was itty-bitty, and the two bedrooms were also small. Yet Nella and Victor's wife, Irene, produced unbelievable feasts from that Lilliputian kitchen. Soups, meats, salads, even caviar, kept coming like rabbits out of the proverbial magician's hat. Mom, Aunt Eleanor and I all looked at each other in astonishment during the lavish feast, wondering in whispered conversation what great expense and mysterious effort Victor and Nella had invested to procure this bounty. The chronic shortages of even basic foodstuffs in the country were well-known. Nella admitted that many of the foods we were eating were delicacies, but, she winked, Viktor worked as a refrigerator technician. He had connections.

Nella spoke English with a heavy accent, yet her command of the language was very sophisticated compared to our paltry Russian phrases and rudimentary Yiddish. I tried to speak to Aunt Rosa as much as I could in Yiddish but was frustrated that I could not get past the most elementary conversations without Nella's help. One day, we had gone on an outing and were on the bus toward home. Aunt Rosa was seated and I stood right next to her, as the bus was crowded. People on the bus were eerily quiet. Though Russians were probably used to this silence on public transportation, I felt it was awkward. In a very quiet voice, I asked Aunt Rosa something in Yiddish. As soon as she heard me begin to speak, she looked at me with a combination of fear and warning, placing her finger over her mouth.

"*In der haim,*" she whispered. *In the house.* I felt so foolish. I should have known that even whispering in a Jewish language in public was dangerous.

When Mom, Aunt Eleanor, and I returned to our hotel late in the evenings, it was clear our privacy had been recklessly trespassed.

Our belongings had been carelessly rummaged through, and we wondered if Sour Svetlana had come back to inspect something she had missed at the airport. No attempt was made to hide the invasion. In fact, microphones hung from the ceiling unapologetically, another friendly reminder that we were unwelcome and were being watched and overheard.

After a week's visit with our family, Mom and Aunt Eleanor flew home. I began the second half of my Soviet adventure and flew to Moscow to join a tour group of the capital and of Leningrad. In Moscow, Lenin's image was everywhere: landscaped into large grassy areas that rose from the street, on statues, on billboards. The unibrowed Premier Leonid Brezhnev's face peered out from other public spaces. The feeling of oppression that had been palpable in Kiev was just as strong in Moscow and Leningrad. The only architecture of any beauty or character had been designed and built decades or centuries before the advent of communism. On the streets, in stores and cafes, I didn't see a single smiling face. My God, no wonder these people drank themselves to death, I thought.

I would have gladly missed the visit to the embalmed Lenin in his mausoleum in Red Square, but on tour, you didn't opt out from this stop to see the waxy dead dictator. Silence was expected and maintained in the long line, which included couples on their wedding day adorned in their nuptial finery. Our tour guide's perverse revisionist history of her country provoked a lot of eye-rolling and elbowing of seat mates, as the tour was mostly comprised of Americans. But one day she made a comment that drove one man apoplectic. We were driving by a monument from World War II when the guide observed that nowadays the Soviet population was able to see that, after the war, Stalin had made . . . (she paused, looking for the right phrase) "a few mistakes."

This middle-aged man had frequently butted heads with the

guide over her fact-challenged presentation of Soviet history. Now he shot up as if fireworks were bursting out of his seat.

"*A few mistakes*?" he screamed. "He murdered tens of millions of people and you call this *a few mistakes*?" Emboldened, other members of the tour began to add their shouts of protest as well. The guide tried to twist her explanations into something that might mollify the angry and incredulous crowd, while avoiding any rendezvous with truth.

I liked to go walking in the evening after the day's tours were over. In the summer the sun didn't go down till after eleven o'clock at night. I felt safe walking alone but took care to follow more or less straight paths so I would not get lost. I walked over Moscow bridges, people-watched, and absorbed the landscape. No one smiled or looked remotely happy. It was eerie. How did people live in such an oppressive society? I guess if I had to wait in three lines in a small store just to purchase an inexpensive jewelry box, and wait in hours-long lines for milk or butter, I'd get depressed too.

One night on my walk a beggar asked me for money. Panhandlers were not supposed to exist in the Soviet Union, where everyone was supposed to have enough money. The next day I asked our tour guide how it was possible there were people on the streets in need of handouts. She looked me straight in the eye and said, "There are no such people in Moscow."

"Yes there are," I said. "I met one last night." I glared at her, only to have her repeat her denial. Did she actually believe what she was saying?

Before leaving Moscow, I wanted to visit a synagogue not too far from my hotel. I had been warned not to do so, told it would probably be locked anyway, and that I shouldn't call attention to myself this way. But with the afterglow from my visit with my family, and with thoughts of Nana and Papa ever-present, I was determined to go to the synagogue. Even if its doors were locked, even if I just stood in front, I would make a statement by paying my respects to a Jewish house of worship. After many wrong turns, the grumpy taxi driver finally found it. I told him to wait for me as I got out. Though it was dusk, normally a time for the afternoon *Mincha* service, the door to the synagogue was locked. I stood on the steps at the entrance for a few minutes and tried to hear the echoes of long-ago prayers that had been offered in this place, an outpouring of appeals to God, maybe even angry, bitter appeals for deliverance from the abuse they suffered in this vast, cold land, and in other lands, simply because they were Jews.

I stood on those steps to the synagogue while the famous dissident hero, Natan Sharansky, was still being held captive in the Siberian gulag, a death penalty hanging over him, simply because he wanted to live freely as a Jew and because he supported the right of others to do so also. Before his arrest, he had regularly met with other dissidents at a Moscow synagogue, and I wondered if this was that same synagogue, where he had first met his wife Avital in 1974 and instantly fallen in love with her. I could not imagine his courage and fierce determination to fight for his freedom to follow his faith, our shared faith, the faith of our ancestors going back more than three thousand years.

Had Nana not made her courageous journey as a teenager, I might have been a refusenik like Natan Sharansky, trying to learn Hebrew with beginning sentences like, "We are Jews but do not know Hebrew," in secret classes using homemade textbooks, comprised of pages they had painstakingly photographed and developed in stealth.

I lived in the freest country the world had ever known, and I was determined not to squander that freedom but to embrace my Jewish identity fully.

Chapter 7

THE GALLERY OF REGRETTABLE DATES

FALL 1983

JEFF ENTERED MY LIFE UNEXPECTEDLY DURING a fleeting season of popularity for me as a single woman. I was twenty-four and totally unaccustomed to my A-list status. For a few weeks I actually had to check my notes about whom I was going out with on which night, and recalled Nana Cohen bragging to me about how much she had been in demand before she married Papa. "Sveetheart, I had to beat them off vit sticks!" she'd say, shaking her head slightly, as if it had been a burden.

I had a dream job as a writer at UCLA Medical Center and loved every minute of it. It was a huge step forward from my first job after college writing for a trade magazine company. It had been awkward at parties to answer the question, "And what do you do?" and have to answer that I wrote for a magazine called *Hospital Gift Shop Management.* This usually led to blank stares and the person I was talking to suddenly remembering he had to make a phone call. I learned to quickly segue to new topics.

Yet for many months after starting my job, I still sat alone in my apartment at night, sobbing, still smarting from a broken heart inflicted after an eight-month relationship with a medical intern had fizzled out. My new series of dates definitely boosted the old self-esteem, but I didn't feel any real sense of connection with any of them. In consolation, I bought myself an expensive, top-of-the-line teddy bear. And after writing about the finer points of hospital gift shop retailing for a year and a half, if there was one thing I had developed an eye for, it was quality teddy bears.

I had fallen in love with the newly minted doctor for reasons both sensible and insensible. First of all, he was a Jewish pediatrician. This meant he cared passionately about children. *So did I!* He was handsome. *I liked handsome men!* He was from Minneapolis, which sounded like a wholesome, friendly place to be from. *I'd buy gloves and a down coat!* He spoke in glowing terms about his parents and sister. *Good sons make good husbands!* Sometimes we made the same jokes at the exact same moment. *Wasn't this destiny?*

But over time, I began to sense trouble. We started to run out of things to talk about during the salad course. He raved about the brilliance of the playwright Harold Pinter and took me to one of his plays. I detested it and the emotional constipation of Pinter's characters. He began to float ideas about expanding our relationship in ways that struck me as decidedly unkosher. (I guess Minneapolis wasn't as wholesome as I had thought!) I tried to swallow my panic. My closest girlfriends all seemed cozily nestled in committed relationships, a few on the verge of engagement. I wanted that security too. I just couldn't figure out how to find the prescription that would make the Doc love me as much as I loved him.

It was a quandary.

When he began excusing himself during dates for short "meditation" breaks, I told myself it wasn't that I was boring him (was I?) but on his grueling, sleep-deprived schedule he couldn't help it. He dropped hints as subtle as a Hummer in a motorcycle showroom that I was about to get dumped but I refused to read the memo. Finally, he began talking about Maggie, whom he had met at the hospital, whose complicated life the Doc found somehow inspiring. When he announced that Maggie had scored two tickets to the Academy Awards and was taking him with her as her date, even I saw that this relationship was going Code Blue, and my crash cart was empty.

I was scared. Handsome pediatric residents who spoke so glowingly about their families and had passionate opinions about the superiority of Huggies over Pampers didn't just drop like chocolate *gelt* from Hanukkah bushes, you know. The young Jewish men I found attractive were either married or gay. I didn't get invited to many parties and was terrified of singles events, though I had never even been to any singles event so my terror was irrational. However, I had not yet been uninvited to attend the Doc's best friend's wedding with him. In a frantic ploy, I spent an entire weekend shopping for a new dress, one that would make the Doc see reason: Wasn't I fabulous? Wasn't I pretty? I felt sucker-punched when I arrived at the wedding hall and found no table card with my name. There was one for The Doctor–"*and Guest.*"

Adding to my humiliation, another woman in the social hall was wearing the exact same new dress I was–the dress that was meant to save my relationship! Now I saw it mirrored on another woman, mocking me. Men think it's funny when they show up somewhere wearing the exact same suit or tie or shirt as another man. They will actually go up to one another to compare their twin outfits, slapping each other on the shoulder because they find it so hilarious. Women who discover a wardrobe twin at a party consider a murder-suicide pact. As I locked eyes with the enemy across the room we understood one another perfectly well: *I'll keep my distance, and you keep yours.*

Doc danced with several attractive women at the wedding while I sat next to his empty seat at the table. When I felt my social immolation nearly complete, I heard the voice of Nana Cohen calling: "Sveetheart, you're not chopped liver! You're a beautiful girl, a *shayna maidel*! He doesn't deserve you!" I realized Nana was right and begged a ride home with another friend.

With the romance now toe-tagged in the relationship morgue, I tried to take comfort in small memories, such as the night the Doc had chastised me for not knowing that respectable bottles of wine have corks and not screw tops. How should I have known? I grew up on Manischewitz! I summoned memories of how often he stopped to admire his reflection in the mirror and his habit of falling into meditative trances when I was in the middle of a sentence. And who wanted to live in Minneapolis anyway? A down coat would just make me look fat.

I was reasonably along in my recovery and blowing through fewer boxes of facial tissue each week when Jeff first called. He introduced himself by explaining that we had a mutual friend in common, Rebecca, whom he had met while living in Jerusalem the previous year. Jeff had just relocated to L.A. from Chicago with his parents and younger sister.

"Rebecca gave me a list of five people to call when I arrived in L.A.," he explained. "She put a star by your name and said I should call you first." We chatted easily for several minutes, and when I said I had to get back to work, he said, "So, do you want to get together so I can see what you look like?"

This was a surprisingly bold question, but Jeff's friendly, gentle tone made it sound merely curious, not arrogant. He also stuttered, which I found strangely endearing. Growing up with a father who was severely hearing-impaired from birth, I had a soft spot for people who had a communication disability. They had to work harder, show more perseverance, and sometimes put up with impatience or intolerance as they tried to be understood. It hadn't hurt that my favorite English professor at UCLA had also been a severe stutterer, the first person I had ever met with this condition. I thought him brave to choose a teaching career, and when he sometimes labored tortuously to release a full word, it hurt me inside.

I suggested to Jeff that we meet at my favorite restaurant in Westwood Village, a casual French bistro. I made sure to show up five minutes late so he'd be the one waiting, not me. I saw him as I approached from down the block, standing outside the restaurant dressed in jeans and a polo shirt. He was nice-looking, slim, tallish, with wavy dark brown hair and glasses. Within two minutes we were talking as if we were old friends, one topic of conversation smoothly streaming into the next with no awkward silences. He startled me by asking me early in the conversation if I had ever been engaged.

"No, have you?" I asked.

He hadn't but told me a story about a woman he had dated for a few weeks in Israel and then broke off the relationship. She had been very intent, in an obvious manner, to try to get Jeff to propose, pronto. After he ended it, she hid her outrage well. But just a few weeks later, she knocked on the door of his dorm room, thrusting her left hand out to show him the engagement ring on her hand. Jeff and I marveled at both her desperation and her determination.

"Good thing you got away when you did!" I laughed.

Jeff wasn't sure what sort of career he was after, but I was already investigating master's programs in journalism and planned to end up in either New York or Chicago the following year for school. Nothing about our first evening out felt like a date–it was too comfortable, too easy. I had the odd sensation that Jeff was not a new person in my life but an old friend whom I simply hadn't met until that evening. And just as I would have with a friend, not a date, I ordered spinach quiche, instructing Jeff to tell me if any got on my teeth.

After dinner we walked through Westwood Village, dipping into Baskin-Robbins, at my suggestion, and each ordering a scoop. I finished my chocolate mint quickly. When Jeff said he was already full and wouldn't finish his, I said, "Hand it over," polishing off his dessert as well. I believe in truth in advertising, so I never pretended that I didn't eat while on dates. *Caveat emptor!*

Inexplicably, it didn't occur to me that we might get together again. After all, he had only said he wanted to get together to see what I looked like. And it had simply felt too natural to have been a date. When I got home that night I thought a little sadly, "What a great guy. Too bad I'll never see him again."

I was thrilled when Jeff called again a week later. Unlike the first time we met, this time he was in a crisp gray suit. *Hey, this guy is good-looking and has nice shoulders*, I realized. About halfway through dinner, with conversation again flowing easily and enjoyably, I had an epiphany: "Maybe this is a real date. Maybe dates don't always have to be awkward!" Jeff had described a disappointing day of job hunting, and I tried to reassure him that with his intelligence, great communication skills, and mature presence, he would soon be employed. At the end of the evening, as we said goodbye, I said, "Call me when you get a job!"

This is what I meant: "I will be so happy when you get a job, I'll want to hear all about it!"

This is what he heard: "*Don't* call me until you get a job, you young punk still living at home with your parents."

I didn't hear from him for a week. Then two weeks. I finally called. He sounded surprised. "I thought you didn't want me to call you until I had a job!"

"What? That's ridiculous!" I was startled to realize my blunder, and we started going out again.

Jeff captured my attention in ways no other young man had before. He told me stories about the road trips he had taken as a boy with his father, a textile salesman, driving through the flat prairie lands of the Midwest from Iowa to Ohio and from Michigan to Central Illinois, visiting textile finishing plants and eating in roadside diners. Bob, Jeff's father, taught him to recognize "quality goods" versus just *shmattes* (rags, in Yiddish). I had never been friends with the jocks in high school and enjoyed hearing Jeff's stories about his own great moments and disappointments on the high school track and baseball teams, the lessons he had learned from his coaches about losing with grace, and about persistence and honor. I had only started jogging in college after I got scared hearing my parents talking to their friends and comparing dosages for the blood pressure medications they were taking. That woke me up to the unpleasant fact that I needed to start exercising and make it a habit.

Less forward by nature than I was, Jeff was entertained when I told him about some of my daring exploits. This included one of my proudest victories: tracking down the home address of my teen idol, the very private Carole King, and riding my bike from the flats of suburban Van Nuys up the twisting, narrow roads of Laurel Canyon to find it. I knocked on her door with my heart knocking in my chest, bearing homemade gifts for her children, which I proffered in abject humility to the young woman who opened the door in surprise. Much more recently, I had connived an assignment to interview Clarence Clemons, the saxophonist in Bruce Springsteen's E Street Band, though I had zero experience writing about music. Jeff admired my penchant to fight for what I felt was right, such as the time I drove around in my tin can of a used car with homemade signs decorated with bright yellow lemons, taped on each side window, to advertise the name of the dealership where I had squandered hard-earned money to buy it.

We also talked about Israel and our experiences there. I had been there twice, both after my bat mitzvah and again for a whole summer when I was sixteen. I had instantly fallen in love with the land and the people, despite Israelis' famous (or infamous) penchant for pushy behavior. Under that sabra (Hebrew for prickly pear cactus, referring to the tough exterior but usually soft interior of native-born Israelis) exterior there was almost always a warm, loving, deeply caring and warm persona waiting to break out, invite you over for dinner, and make sure you wore a sweater at night when you left.

Jeff had grown up attending a Reform synagogue in a Chicago suburb, and his year in Israel, both discovering his religious roots and working part-time at a research institute, spurred him to further exploration. Reminding me of my friend Steve from the *Havurat No'ar* program in junior high school, Jeff said, "I'm learning at my own pace, but I know that following the Torah will be the key to living a more meaningful life than the one I grew up with." He had even taken the step of attending an Orthodox shul on the Venice boardwalk called Pacific Jewish Center.

I considered myself too modern to be affiliated in any way with Orthodoxy and was uncomfortable with Jeff's Orthodox leanings. On the other hand, I liked him too much to stop dating him over it. He made me laugh with his ironic jokes and Monty Python imitations. His spiritual quest made me think, for the first time seriously, about setting spiritual goals for my life, beyond just professional goals. I had to admit, I had never given the idea of setting spiritual goals a thought.

As much as I liked Jeff, though, he was young, unemployed, and living at home. He hardly seemed like husband material at the moment. We were not dating each other exclusively, but after a series of very dreadful dates with other men in rapid succession, I reconsidered waiting for Jeff, even if he needed a year or two to want to get serious.

For example, a well-meaning colleague pushed me hard to go out on a blind date with a friend of hers because we were both Jewish and she, a Catholic, considered this enough of a reason to foist the idea on us both. When we met it was instantly clear we had nothing to say to one another, yet so much time in which not to say it. A different guy, on our first and last date, immediately snapped the restaurant menu open even as we waited in the restaurant foyer for our table, not even looking at me. The choices of soup and salad must have been mesmerizing.

The final straw was my last date with "Brad," whom I had been seeing for a few weeks. He was bright, sweet, and sensitive, and in school to become a Reform rabbi. Yet my Cohen DNA asserted itself, and I felt my religious views were too traditional for the role of a Reform rabbi's wife. This was totally absurd, because I didn't keep Shabbos or even keep strictly kosher. If anything, Brad honored more traditions than I did, keeping a semblance of Shabbos observance. However, when Brad tested his sermons out on me, I was completely underwhelmed by their lack of depth. I was on the verge of telling Brad I could not see him anymore when he called me early one Sunday morning.

"Judy, you've got to come with me next Saturday night to the most amazing experience! I went last night and I can hardly describe it, but it's totally transformative." He promised it was deep and profound, and might change the way I see *everything*.

It sounded intriguing, but I turned him down. I wanted to spend next Saturday night with Jeff, whom I was sure would ask me out. Brad refused to take no for an answer, and against my wiser instincts I relented. Brad took me to a cold, cavernous hall in a poorly lit, industrial part of Santa Monica. I felt a little queasy.

Where had he brought me? What was all this about? We joined the line of other people signing liability waivers for any injury, emotional distress, or accidental death or dismemberment that might ensue from the evening's mysterious raptures. Against all sense, I signed it. We were ushered into a large dark room with about fifty other people. A group leader instructed us all to stand closely opposite someone we didn't know. I stood facing a tall man wearing a button that had a long German name on it.

I asked, "Who is Shmidttenglockmann?" (Or something like that, something long and German.)

"You've never heard of Shmidttenglockmann?" He looked at me as if I had confessed that I had never heard of marijuana. His tone and expression were imperious. "Why, Shmidttenglockmann is only the most important painter of the modern age."

After that introduction, the Art Snob and I played a mirroring game, an activity I hadn't indulged in since I was a kid at day camp. Art Snob's focused expression confirmed that he was totally absorbed in this game, and I felt my blood begin to boil. As we were instructed to play one moronic game after another my frustration brought me to tears. I had never been so desperate to escape from any place as I was that night, but who do you call for help when you are held hostage by organizers of pseudo-profound, touchy-feely trust exercises?

I knew I had hit rock bottom–almost literally–when I dropped to the floor to crawl on all fours, meowing like a cat. Every fiber of my being was in mutiny over this tragically misspent evening. I was furious with myself for having lacked the courage to just say no to Brad, and I was too afraid of the neighborhood to run out of the place and wait for him, alone. Brad had been right about one thing, though: I now saw everything differently in terms of my relationship with him. It was over. "I could have been out with Jeff!" I thought as I meowed, feeling I was being justly punished for having ditched him that evening. I also couldn't wait to tell him about this insanity. I already imagined how we'd laugh about it together.

As soon as we were released from captivity, seemingly days later, I ran outside, fuming. Brad looked at me with bright, shining eyes and a broad smile. "What did you think?"

I issued a stream of salty invective, uncharacteristically venomous. Kinder, more G-rated words would have included balderdash, tripe, superficial, absurd, and idiotic. Nana would have accurately called it *narishkeit*. Brad looked aggrieved and could not understand why I found the evening's employments to be anything less than transformative. I was shocked when Brad still wanted to date me after my temper tantrum. I had to give the man credit for trying, but he was not my Mr. Right or Rabbi Right.

I never wanted to turn down an invitation to go out with Jeff again. The problem was, his experiences in Israel had changed the trajectory of his life. And as a result, our fledgling relationship was on a collision course.

Chapter 8

GROWING CONFLICT

1983–1984

As a teenager, Jeff had begun to examine his family's lifestyle. He had looked at the two-story suburban home, the safe neighborhood, the late-model cars and dinners out, and then observed to his dad, "This is all very nice, but there must be more to life than this. There has to be!" The question didn't make sense to his father, Robert Gruen (born Lothar Gruenebaum), who had been plucked out of Nazi Germany as a five-year-old in 1938 and had lived through a poor and lonely childhood in Washington Heights, New York. Bob, as he became known, had found purpose and happiness as a husband and father of three children and as a successful salesman. Like many immigrants who almost cannot believe their good fortune in being able to live safely and even thrive economically in their adopted nation, Bob was more bewildered than intrigued by his son's existential questions.

But during a trip to Israel during a spring break from his Junior Year Abroad program at Lancaster University in England, people finally offered some answers to Jeff's questions. On a lark, Jeff agreed to stay for a few days at a yeshiva called Aish HaTorah to try out some classes. The days turned into a few weeks, and the yeshiva's charismatic founding teacher, a born-and-bred New Yorker named Rabbi Noah Weinberg, directly challenged students to answer the question: "What are you living for?" Rabbi Weinberg taught that the Torah not only had the answers to what life was about, but also showed how Torah study and observance could lead to a life of meaning, purpose, and happiness. He taught that living this way was the Jews' mandate, encouraging his students to engage in Jewish study and practice. "Don't just be part of the 'Chosen People' but part of the *choosing people*," he said.

One Friday night, in a hall filled with more than a hundred students and teachers, Jeff serendipitously ended up sitting next to Rabbi Weinberg at dinner. He was startled when the jovial, approachable rabbi took his hand and held it gently for a few moments. No words were spoken.

Recalling that night, Jeff told me, "Rabbi Weinberg had an uncanny sense of where people were coming from. He intuited that I was feeling insecure and uncertain about all of these new ideas. On the other hand, I felt like I was coming home."

All the talk about God, the Jewish role in history, why individual actions mattered, and the profound impact of doing mitzvot (commandments) overwhelmed him. "I felt that what I was hearing was true, though part of me didn't want them to be true," he explained to me one night when we were walking on the quiet streets near his parents' home in Santa Monica. "No one had ever before presented to me an articulate paradigm that demonstrated what life was meant to be about. No one had ever before asked me, 'Where do you get your core values from?' The ideas were upending so many of my ideas about my life and how I should live it. It was too intense, and I almost felt sick. I realized I had to leave as soon as possible."

Back at Lancaster University, he began reading Jewish history and philosophy and, over time, began to partially observe Shabbos. He found this process simultaneously exciting, confusing, compelling, and threatening. By the time Jeff and I met, he had found his equilibrium and was attending Pacific Jewish Center's synagogue on the Venice boardwalk, led by a charismatic Orthodox rabbi named Daniel Lapin.

I had seen almost from the beginning that Jeff could be that special man who would never let me feel lonely on Valentine's Day, my birthday, or any other day. We talked easily about so many things, and had the same sense of humor. Yet after only a few weeks of dating, he made me jittery by tossing out big religious questions:

How often did I think about God?

Did I think about whether the Torah was true or not?

Did I think that Jewish law should change according to the times, or did I think I should design my life to align with traditional Jewish values, even if it put me out of step with the prevailing culture?

These were seriously unnerving questions. No one had ever asked me anything like them before. Weren't these questions only for rabbis or theology students? My stomach started to knot up. A little religion was good, but too much wasn't. I saw that our ideas of how to define what was "enough" religion would diverge quickly.

One day, he brought up the topic of Shabbos. He said that he loved the idea that for one day a week he wasn't thinking about work or identifying himself by his career. "It's a time to just be, let the rest of the world stay the way it is. I like having time to try to connect to who I really am, and where I'm going, and focus on connecting to something larger, to God."

I usually spent my Saturdays doing errands, shopping, lunching with friends, catching a movie, or writing. Of course I saw the appeal of having a holy day dedicated to higher pursuits–theoretically–but

I had never been a spiritual seeker and found myself lost in this new thought territory.

I squirmed inside, realizing that my lack of curiosity about these Big Picture questions didn't reflect well on me. I wanted Jewish values to inform my life and believed they already did. I was a "nice" and "good" person, I thought. I felt confident that those impulses came from core Jewish values. But Jeff's prodding startled me into recognizing I needed to give these questions more attention. I began to see that without a baseline definition of "good," or "justice," or "fairness," everything ethically and morally was up for grabs, depending on changing cultural whims. After all, in Victorian England they thought that sending children to work in boot-blacking factories was a good idea. In the 1970s, some people decided that "open marriages," with spouse-swapping for an evening's frivolity was just naughty fun. My fears and insecurities from being a child in the 1960s also showed how quickly society can change–sometimes for the worse. The idea of having some immutable standards given by an omniscient, omnipotent God started sounding like a better idea.

While I was threatened by these philosophical questions, my attention was easily and enthusiastically engaged when Jeff started sharing what he was learning about the Hebrew language. I had enjoyed my Hebrew language classes from high school and had retained a fair amount of it. Rabbi Lapin called Hebrew "the Lord's language," showing how it revealed truths about life. For example, the word for "friend" in Hebrew is *yedid* (ye-*deed*), spelled with the repeating two letters: *yud* and *dalet.* One set of *yud-dalet* spells *yad* or hand. *Yedid*, therefore, is literally spelled as if to say "hand in hand," expressing the closeness of friendship. Similarly, the Hebrew word for face is *panim* (pa-*neem*), which is a plural construction. Not only does everybody have different faces they project in different circumstances, but the word is also related to the word *p'neem*, which means "inside." Whichever face a person is showing, it reflects their inner feelings at that moment. I wanted to learn more about how Hebrew revealed truths about life.

No one in Jeff's family was particularly interested in what he was learning at Rabbi Lapin's Thursday night classes, so Jeff was keen to share his new insights with me, frequently asking what I thought about them.

I was struggling with these new ideas of Judaism for multiple reasons. I didn't want to admit how much my inner conflict was growing. I was also confused by my own resistance to these ideas. All my life I had chosen to be involved with Jewish activities like my synagogue youth group, the synagogue drama group, working as a teacher's assistant in its Hebrew School and as assistant youth director. I also chose to live a culturally Jewish life by living in a Jewish sorority in college and even directed my earliest journalism efforts to the Jewish media. I was certain I would not intermarry and I believed in Israel as the Jewish homeland.

I realized that until now, all my Jewish involvement had been more emotional and cultural than religious. I was pretty sure the God of Israel existed, but I flicked away concerns about whether He had any particular expectations of me. I didn't even pray, and surely didn't read the Torah's weekly chapters.

I also considered myself a feminist, and I was certain that was the opposite of Orthodox. True, I had once attended a conference of Orthodox Jewish feminists in New York, so I knew such a category existed. The women there discussed hot-button issues such as women reading publicly from the Torah, women as rabbis, and how to gain more public roles for Orthodox women, but I found even these Orthodox feminists too much for me. The married ones kept their hair covered, and wore skirts instead of pants. Their fight was not my fight.

But I was no longer capable of staying comfortable in my current practice of emotional Jewish identity with almost zero Jewish practice: Jeff was presenting new and profound ideas to me which resonated within me as being true and valuable. Even if we broke up, it was too late to "unhear" these ideas.

While I liked thinking of myself as a fighter, I seemed only to be fighting against something, but not *for* anything. I had to face the distressing fact that the reality of who I was did not match the exalted sense of myself as fair-minded and Jewishly committed–me, the supposedly open-minded modern woman who refused to even attend a class taught by an Orthodox rabbi!

With every passing week, Jeff's education with Rabbi Lapin convinced him more and more that he wanted a life that integrated Jewish practice into his daily life, like what he saw being modeled in the Pacific Jewish Center community.

"I'm convinced that God gave the Torah to the Jewish people at Mount Sinai, and I'm convinced that if I follow it as best I can, I'll have the best chance of building a successful marriage and family life," he told me. "I don't want my kids to ask me, 'What else is there besides the next vacation or the next new car?' and not have an answer, like my dad didn't have an answer for me. I want a life that is about something bigger than I am, something that will be deep and spiritually rich and eternal."

I swallowed hard and asked myself some tough questions: Can this relationship be saved? Could I still have a happy marriage and a successful family if I lived with less spiritual integrity? Was I being shallow by resisting God's blueprint for Jewish living?

You're not shallow, I could hear Papa Rosenfeld say. *There is no God. You're an educated young woman. Don't fall for fairy tales.*

The Torah is true, argued the voice of Papa Cohen from heaven. *We came to America for freedom, but look what happened: we went too far in relaxing the standards–almost no one in your generation keeps Shabbos anymore. Go back to our traditions!*

I continued to resist Jeff's invitations to attend Rabbi Lapin's classes, leery of his reputation as an authoritarian figure but intrigued by his fiercely independent streak. Unlike "normal" rabbis who earned a salary for their pulpit duties, Rabbi Lapin ran a business to support his growing family, refusing a salary from the synagogue he served to maintain his autonomy from the board of directors. He defined membership at Pacific Jewish Center not through a check but through a commitment to attendance at his weekly classes. If you couldn't attend, you were expected to call. I didn't like this controlling style, which only aggravated my internal conflict.

A former Berkeley roommate of mine had once gone to one of his classes and reported that Rabbi Lapin's ideas were comically antiquated and that after the class men and women ended up speaking in single-sex groups, where she overheard some young married women talking quietly among themselves about their pregnancies. It was her first and last class.

Based on this report about Rabbi Lapin and his group of devotees, I had thought, "You'll never catch me with those kinds of people!" But who were "those kinds of people?" In reality, they were mostly people like Jeff and me: middle-class Jews who had been raised with Jewish educations so shallow that even after years of Hebrew School we were hard-pressed to name all the Ten Commandments.

Deep down, I was always relieved that Orthodox Jews were still around. I suspected that there was truth in the Torah and that keeping the commandments was important. I simply preferred that they continue to do the heavy lifting so that I could keep going to the mall on Saturdays. In fact, I often drove past groups of religious Jews on Saturdays as they walked home from synagogue in my Pico-Robertson neighborhood, an area whose religious population was booming. Embarrassed, I crouched low behind the steering wheel so they wouldn't see me breaking Shabbos.

As my resistance to attending Rabbi Lapin's class was cracking, and Jeff introduced yet another God conversation, I burst out, "Why can't we just go to the movies like other couples and talk about that? Or how about the latest scandal with the British royal family? I'd settle for a talk about fluctuating interest rates! This is too much religious talk for me."

"Okay, I understand," he said. "But you have to realize, this whole dimension of spirituality has been missing for my whole life. Until I knew it existed, I didn't even know it was missing! Nobody had been around to show me. Work can only provide so much conversation. And how long can you talk about a movie? I'll talk about other things, but you need to do the same. Want to go to a movie tonight?" he asked, grinning.

All this tension would have been bad enough for someone who found the word "Torah" fraught with unbearable weightiness and antiquity, but one evening as we were taking a walk after dinner, an unexpected new barrier arose. It was 1984, and Ronald Reagan had recently been reelected president. I noticed a Reagan-Bush '84 bumper sticker on a passing car and said, "Every time I see a bumper sticker like that, I wonder: What could that person have been thinking?" No sooner had the words flown from my mouth than I felt the anchor dropping and pulling me down: Although we had not discussed politics, I suddenly knew that not only was this guy an aspiring religious fanatic, he was also a Republican! Why was there always a fatal flaw in every guy I liked?

Confirming my fears, Jeff said in a quiet voice, "I voted for Reagan."

I couldn't believe it. Wasn't it enough that I had to wrestle with the prospect of possibly becoming Orthodox, which to me meant a future of dressing like it was the 1950s (maybe the 1850s) and trying to reconcile my feminist beliefs with what I envisioned as a second-class status–of living among people I assumed would all share a groupthink mentality? Jeff's spiritual quest and our discussions about what God wanted from the Jewish people were already rocking my worldview. I could have cut and run, but I had too much respect for what Jeff was trying to achieve in his life. I loved spending time with him–most of the time–and if I was serious about wanting real Jewish substance in my life I'd actually have to do something to make sure it would be there. Jeff offered me a path. Could we find a middle ground between his nascent Orthodoxy and my Conservative liberalism?

The evening opened up another front in our battleground of ideas. Jeff explained why he had voted for the "rich white man's party," as I saw it, and we argued about the merits of various social welfare and educational policies. We argued over the Head Start program, which I supported because it was for little children. But when he asked me if I would still support Head Start if it had proven to be monstrously costly and duplicative and had a miserably low success rate in advancing the educational outcomes of poor children, I had no answer. Grudgingly, I realized I might need more facts at hand for future conversations.

My first fear after learning that Jeff had voted for Reagan wasn't even whether he had been right or wrong in doing so–it was that my friends might find out about it. Dating a non-Jew would have raised eyebrows among my friends, but dating a Republican would mark me as an outcast for life. Jews were Democrats–everybody knew that! I didn't even know any Jewish Republicans, except now, this very special one.

I schemed about ways to keep Jeff's political affiliation a secret, as if he worked for the CIA and I was sworn to secrecy about what he did. Other than religion–and now politics–Jeff was perfect: kind, honest, ethical, intelligent, caring, funny, hardworking. We had a lot of fun together, going out for Sunday brunches, having dinner with our growing circle of friends, hiking, hanging out, going to movies. Despite our theological arguments, we actually viewed life in much the same way, and we shared a sense of the ridiculous. He also challenged my stereotyping of the Orthodox world: if Orthodox Jewish men were sexist, why was he showing me so much respect for my achievements and ambition? Why was he putting up with my relentless arguing?

I wanted a *mentsch* for a husband–a good, sensitive, honest man. Jeff showed me in every way that he would always be kind, gentle, and loyal. He was good to his mother and faithfully kept breakfast dates with his eighty-year-old grandmother every Tuesday. He was polite and gracious to waiters, which I had read in a magazine was an important clue to a person's manners and ego.

He wasn't exactly perfect, though. He ate agonizingly slowly, prompting my mother to whisper to me in the kitchen the first night Jeff had dinner with us, "When is he ever going to finish that plate?" We Rosenfelds dispatched our meals as if we were going to miss the last train out of the shtetl before the Cossacks arrived. We were not used to a guest eating at such a relaxed, almost negligent pace. I would try to get him to pick up the pace. His other flaw was occasionally committing random acts of painfully corny humor; prompting me to grit my teeth and wait for the next, higher-level wry aside. But when I looked at the balance sheet, I wasn't giving him up so fast.

"The Reagan revelation" forced me to face an uncomfortable truth–namely, that my definition of what was "important" in life had been limited. While politics, family, friendships, Israel were all important, the idea of a spiritual life hadn't landed on my radar screen until Jeff introduced it to me. I was coming to see that without it, life would be missing a profound dimension.

I was frustrated and confused: if we had so much in common when we discussed issues such as family life, friends, career goals, literature, music, and how we interpreted various day-to-day situations, could our core values be that far apart? Was I already a secret religious and political conservative but didn't know it? I shuddered inside.

It had been nearly a dozen years since I had been concerned enough about the question of God's existence to make that appointment with my synagogue rabbi. Now at twenty-four, I had to ask myself: would I remain a spiritual adolescent for the rest of my life? My sense of personal honesty and intellectual integrity left me no choice: I had to attend one of Rabbi Lapin's classes with Jeff and for the first time hear about Jewish teachings from a source steeped in authentic Torah lessons.

However, as much as I liked Jeff and saw potential in our future, I remained determined that the decisions I made about how I lived my life would be authentically mine.

Chapter 9

MEETING RABBI LAPIN

SPRING 1985

IN THE SPRING I RECEIVED THE OVERSIZED, fat envelope holding my acceptance to the Medill School of Journalism at Northwestern. I was thrilled and Jeff seemed relieved. After I'd gone, he'd get a break from my *hocking a chainik* (Yiddish for pestering, literally, "banging a tea kettle"). I assumed he would look for a more religious and less contrary girlfriend when I left town. Who could blame him? Our outings sometimes seemed more like debate team practices than dates. With one foot figuratively out the door, I went with Jeff to my first Thursday night Torah class in Rabbi Lapin's home.

The Lapins' living room and dining room area was packed with about fifty men and women sitting on folding chairs. Sweeping the room with my eyes, I studied the women's heads, silently counting the number of "open-air" uncovered heads versus those wearing wigs (although great wigs can fool you), scarves, or other head coverings. Most Orthodox married women covered their hair in public, and that was one law I knew I could never abide. I was glad to see some women who appeared to be both married and bareheaded. As I sat down next to Jeff, I felt my jaw clench reflexively. For Jeff's sake I wanted to like Rabbi Lapin and this whole new world of Torah study and observance, but because the rabbi was both Orthodox and a white South African, I assumed he was racist and sexist, so I also really didn't want to like him.

In a well-cut gray suit and tie, Rabbi Lapin smiled and nodded at the people filing in. Presiding at a lectern in front of the fireplace, I noticed the bookshelves on either side of him were crowded with classic titles of English literature, a multi-volume history of Winston Churchill, and books about physics and nautical navigation. I had assumed his library might be Hebrew and Aramaic-only. After all, my own Papa Cohen, who wasn't even Orthodox, had bookshelves filled mostly with Talmudic tomes. I had assumed that Orthodoxy meant "narrow," and it was crucial to me that any Orthodox rabbi I listened to was broadly educated.

The Lapins' three daughters, ages two to five, sat in pint-sized rocking chairs in their pajamas next to their father. They were scene-stealing adorable, all with luminous blue eyes and blond hair. If all the other kids in this community were going to be this cute, I would fold like a weak poker hand. The living and dining room also opened to the kitchen, and alluring aromas wafted through the house as Rabbi Lapin's wife, Susan, cooked for *Shabbos* while listening to his class. What a surprise, I thought with a bit of irritation: the wife's in the kitchen; the husband's the star of the show.

Rabbi Lapin was a natural teacher, charismatic, exuberant, and commanding. That night he described the dramatic scene when the elderly patriarch Isaac plans to bequeath the blessing of the firstborn to Esau, the elder of his twin sons. Isaac has instructed Esau to "hunt some game" and prepare a meal for him before he gives the blessing. Apparently, this blessing of the firstborn is a very big deal. Whoever gets that prize also gets to pass down the spiritual DNA needed to forge Jewish destiny throughout the millennia.

But Isaac's wife, Rebecca, has other ideas and intervenes. She commands the younger twin, Jacob, to appear before Isaac and pose as Esau, presenting him with a meal she will prepare. Each parent has a favorite son, and Jacob is Rebecca's. She is convinced that this quieter and more reflective son must have the blessing.

This family feud could get nasty, I think, sitting and listening. This Esau is a rough guy, a hunter with a famous rap sheet for womanizing, theft, and even murder. I can see where Rebecca is coming from on this one, and Esau's personality is one she understands better than her husband, because she is the sister and daughter of men seasoned in the arts of deception. Both Isaac and Rebecca see that Esau could become a leader, theoretically, but only Rebecca understands that his potential for leadership will always be dwarfed by his bloodlust. With a goatskin on his arm, Jacob tries to pass himself off as his hairier, coarser brother when he stands before his nearly blind father. Jacob hadn't liked this stratagem and protested, pointing out the trickery involved and the risk of discovery. But even in the book of Genesis, mother knows best, and Rebecca insists that Jacob go through with the deception and assumes all responsibility for any price to be paid.

Jacob manages to convince his skeptical father that he is Esau, and receives the powerful, history-changing blessing. When Esau arrives shortly after, prepared with the meal he has hunted and cooked to his father's specifications, he discovers the deception. He cries out bitterly: "Do you not have a blessing for me?" It's a heartbreaking scene. His father loved him, and chose to see his son's potential more than his manifest flaws. Through her behind-the-scenes maneuvering, the matriarch Rebecca changes the course of Jewish history.

I was spellbound by the story. How had I never learned about this momentous episode through so many years of synagogue attendance and after-school Jewish education? I was shocked just trying to imagine this family living out such a tumultuous power play. Rabbi Lapin's discussion showed that the biblical first families were actual flesh-and-blood people, with achingly poignant problems, conflicts, dreams, even marital disputes. In Hebrew school, biblical personalities had been presented as distant, fairy-tale characters.

I tried to follow along as Rabbi Lapin dissected the text line by line, revealing deeper layers of meaning as well as curiosities and inconsistencies in the Hebrew, a language whose exquisite distinctions I had never realized. These linguistic nuances of the text are hard enough to catch even if you are fluent in Hebrew. They are absolutely impossible to see reading a translation–any translation. Learning the text "inside," he pointed out odd grammar and syntax, mismatched tenses, seemingly random jumps in the storyline, double entendres, and other clues to help unravel the mysteries of the biblical narrative.

For my entire life I had been passionate about the written word. I read and wrote in nearly all my spare time. I felt fortunate that I had a career where I could focus on and explore the world of language, always seeking more imaginative, precise, and evocative ways to tell a story, summon emotions, or make people laugh. As a journalist, I also loved figuring out what questions to ask that would reveal the story I needed to tell. That night I was jolted by the realization that the way Rabbi Lapin taught Torah had a lot in common with investigative journalism: he was digging for truth by asking why this unusual word was used instead of another, more common word; what message was being sent when the storyline was suddenly out of order; what the significance was of seeing a particular word used for the very first time. There were meaningful answers to all these questions. It took patient digging to find out the answers. Given all this, I knew I could not resist delving deeper to learn what these Hebrew words meant, and as a good journalist tries to do, to find the story behind the story.

Examining the text so minutely and deeply, it was no wonder that while Rabbi Lapin had already been teaching the Five Books of Moses for seven years, he was not yet quite halfway through Genesis in this weekly ninety-minute class. Sitting in this class was like going on a literary archeology dig, with this formidable and formal rabbi as our guide. It was obvious that he loved teaching, and was enthusiastically in command not only of the material but also of the dynamics in the room. He quoted several famous Torah commentators, and I saw from reading the text notes that they had lived anywhere from five hundred to twelve-hundred years earlier. Other than Rashi, who lived in the late 11th century in France, I had never heard of any of them.

My first class with Rabbi Lapin also revealed how little I really knew about Judaism, even after so many years of active participation in Jewish educational life. I began to feel embarrassed at the misplaced confidence I had in my knowledge. In truth, my Jewish IQ was probably lower than that of a potato knish. But since Rabbi Lapin's students were comprised nearly entirely of people with similar backgrounds to Jeff's and mine, I felt comfortable to return the following week, and the week after that, and the week after that. We'd frequently go out for coffee afterward to talk about the class, and for the first time in my life I was learning classic, unapologetic, unadulterated Jewish thought about society, psychology, Jewish destiny, and the different roles mapped out for men and women. Everything else I had heard until this point had gone through a filter of some sort of reforming philosophy and interpretation; this was the real ancient deal, without any overlay of 20th century attitudes.

I remained vigilant in my eagerness to seize on areas of disagreement with Rabbi Lapin, and I found plenty, especially his opinions about men's and women's roles, which I found to be sexist and narrow. On the other hand, I was struck to have learned that the matriarch Rebecca, who would not have counted in an Orthodox minyan, was praised by the ancient commentators when she took matters into her own hands to alter the rest of Jewish destiny. Her understanding in this realm was greater than her husband's.

I was also jarred by the extreme deference of Rabbi Lapin's audience to everything he said. Everyone seemed in awe of him, and I was suspicious. Was this what a cult looked like? It would have been tempting to try to pigeonhole Rabbi Lapin as some benighted religious scholar, but his intellectual rigor and scope made that impossible. I had to pay very close attention to try and follow the links he made between what was happening in the lives of the patriarchs and matriarchs and such disparate topics as Newtonian physics, the poetry of Byron, the economic theories of Adam Smith, and strategies for navigating a sailboat from California to Hawaii, something he had personally done with his young family. This was not stream of consciousness. This was a brilliant weaving together of history, science, literature, and Talmudic thought, and he made it all coalesce. If you wanted to follow, your synapses needed to fire on all cylinders.

I kept my new habit of attending the classes under wraps. No need to blab to anyone that I was actually checking out Orthodox Judaism. Soon, I came down with a case of what Rabbi Lapin accurately diagnosed as cognitive dissonance. Many of his points struck me in some primal way as being true, but all my intellectual and emotional static made them hard to hear. My Jewish education had taught me some of the fundamentals: that we must pursue justice, perform acts of kindness, and give charity. But in a world of rapidly changing definitions of morality, Rabbi Lapin asked questions I had not considered.

"Who would you rather have define what constitutes a just society, God Himself or some committee of eggheads who first tested their standards in a political focus group?" Rabbi Lapin asked. Over endless cups of coffee, Jeff and I debated Lapinesque ideas: are some acts of kindness actually cruel? Who defines the fair amount of taxation or of charity?

My upbringing in the Conservative movement had taught me that Judaism had to change with the times to remain relevant. I was proud of this selling point. Conservative Judaism seemed progressive without giving away the store, as I considered the Reform movement had done by making everything the Torah had commanded optional. Change suggested enlightenment, adaptability, and progress–who could argue with that? But I also saw the results coming in, and they troubled me: Intermarriage was skyrocketing except among the Orthodox, signaling an apathy for traditional Jewish values. It was also easy to see that in my generation, people were losing the emotional and religious ties to Judaism that our parents, even fairly secular ones, had retained. My Cohen grandparents had failed to inspire a commitment to traditional Jewish practice in their children or most of their grandchildren, despite their heartfelt efforts. Among their grandchildren, I had been most receptive to their message, yet even I wasn't a regular Shabbos observer. This made me sad.

Although I often sat scowling during class, alert to pounce on ideas that struck me as illiberal, I couldn't fight the dawning sense that Rabbi Lapin had important, transcendent lessons to teach me. In fact, I was whipsawed by how many of my unquestioned assumptions he delighted in turning on their heads. For example, he claimed that a life based on God-given restrictions and discipline was the path to true freedom, a lesson I never heard at UC Berkeley. He taught that what he called "ethical capitalism" was not only expedient but moral, because in a free society people can only make money by supplying things that other people want. But because people so easily get carried away by greed, we have the words "In God We Trust" on our currency as a reminder to maintain

God-given ethical standards. Just try testing these ideas out on your secular Jewish friends and see how many you have left at the end of the evening.

I had a lot of questions for Rabbi Lapin and began standing in line after classes to ask about things I didn't understand. One of my first "newbie" questions prompted a startling answer.

"Why do you say 'Rashi says' instead of 'Rashi said,' given that he lived in the 12th century?" I asked.

"Rashi is as alive today as he was when he lived in the Middle Ages," Rabbi Lapin explained. "His insights are almost unmatched for their clarity and depth, and he is studied more than ever before in history." Other luminaries who helped "decode" Torah text, whether they lived three hundred years ago or fifteen hundred years ago, are similarly granted "present tense" status. This helped me appreciate why the Five Books of Moses were frequently referred to as "the Living Torah."

One night we were invited to the Lapins' home for Shabbos dinner. I was a little nervous, unsure how the social dynamics would work and still very uncertain about my participation in an Orthodox community. The table was set with fine china and elegant wine goblets, and there were a few other guests in addition to Jeff and me. Rabbi Lapin appeared more genial and relaxed than I was used to seeing on Thursday nights. He and Susan were gracious hosts, ably engaging their guests in conversation. I felt another chip in my armor fall away as I observed the rabbi's open and ardent admiration for his wife, an extremely intelligent and accomplished woman in her own right.

At one point during the conversation, one guest asked, "Come on, Rabbi, don't you really want all the people who come to your Torah classes to become religious like you are?"

"Not at all," he said. "I'm here to show what the Torah says about how to live a successful life. I believe that there is an intuitive hunger in the human soul for timeless ideas. People value many things because they are old, which is why you have retro chic and antique collectibles. These days, it's rarer to find teachers who are transmitting old ideas that people sense are valuable. I'm teaching what I am convinced is the most soul-nourishing idea of all, about God. After that, people will obviously make up their own minds. I'm simply offering them an important option to consider."

After several weeks of attending the class, I agreed to go to PJC's synagogue for Shabbos services. It was an unlikely outpost for a Jewish Orthodox renaissance. The shul's neighbors included tattoo parlors, hip cafés, alternative bookstores, and a drug rehab center. It was not unusual for the drug-addled to stumble in, or for the shirtless on roller skates to zoom in from the boardwalk. In fact, one member of the community had made his first entry on Shabbos using just this mode of transportation.

I felt my heart thudding loudly as we walked into the shul, and I was welcomed warmly by Michael Medved, the founding president of the PJC community and already a renowned author and movie critic, who deftly escorted me to the women's section. I appreciated his friendly smile as I tried to decide if coming to a separate-seating synagogue demonstrated an admirable, if hard-won open-mindedness or simply made me a sellout.

I had vowed never to visit a synagogue with separate seating. Now I felt I had somehow crossed the Rubicon. I felt awkward and a little frightened, and appreciated the many warm smiles and nods that greeted me. Sensing my newbie status, someone handed me the siddur, or prayer book, opened to the page where the service was about to begin. At least I can read the Hebrew, I thought with relief, but the service covered much more than I was used to, and my reading skills were too rudimentary to keep up. When the congregation got up to sing "Lecha Dodi," which welcomes the "Shabbos Bride," I sang along, grateful for the familiar tune.

The summer flew. Before I knew it I was boarding my flight for Chicago, a tear-sodden mess. I was no longer so sure that I wanted to leave. At the airport, Jeff tried to divert me from my breakdown by pointing to the colorful weather map in *USA Today*, where Chicago was sunny and a pleasant seventy-two degrees. It was no use. I had sudden and desperate buyer's remorse over my decision to leave L.A. I had an enviable job as a writer, a nice apartment, a boyfriend, my family, girlfriends, a full life. All of which I would be trading in for a dumpy dorm room in a town where I knew only one person (barely) to get a degree that–if I was lucky–would enable me to get the kind of job I already had. Was I totally meshuga? So many of my friends had gone off to various grad school programs, I wondered if I had just followed along, sheep-like, chasing another piece of sheepskin that I didn't need. I walked down the Jetway like a zombie, crying even harder once Jeff was out of sight because, frankly, he seemed a little too chipper at my departure. What if he replaced me quickly? What if I never met anyone else as kind and intelligent and funny as he was?

Fortunately, Chicago showed itself to glorious advantage the day I arrived. It was cool, with clouds billowing against a gorgeous blue sky. This was my first time in the Midwest, and Evanston was a beautiful little college town. As expected, my dorm room was tiny and gloomy. The dull walls hadn't seen fresh paint in years and were pockmarked by sprays of tiny holes where posters had been pinned throughout the ages. The view from my window was of the dreary parking lot and the Maple Street "El" train stop. I pined for my L.A. apartment and its third-floor view of a pretty, tree-lined street. My roommate had left photos of herself in the minuscule entry hall, heavily made up and dressed in scanty party attire. We were a serious mismatch, I concluded.

Unlike the cushy pace I had enjoyed in the world of university public relations, in grad school we had from 8:30 a.m. till 4 p.m. to identify a newsworthy topic, research it, track down sources, write the story, and turn it in. We were all typing furiously from 3:30 onward; anyone still typing at 4:02 need not bother handing in the assignment. I thrived on the adrenaline rush of it all. I loved calling up complete strangers to ask questions about topics that would otherwise be none of my business if I were not a journalist. I sifted through the latest legal filings in Chicago's downtown courthouse, scouting for stories before I hit the pavement again in the bracing cold January winds that taught me to leave my open-toed shoes in my dorm room and invest in warm boots at Marshall Field's. I also sold two humor essays to the *Chicago Tribune*, which made me do the happy dance.

I still had plenty of time to troll Evanston's wonderful bookstores, like the proverbial kid in a candy shop, and walking along Sheridan Road, which hugs the campus. I was smitten by the novelty of the Prairie-style mansions along Lake Michigan, on expansive lots with million-dollar views of the lake.

While I was not eager to date anyone else, I reluctantly accepted a dinner invitation from a man I met in town. As soon as we met at the restaurant I had a bad feeling about him. He was tense, the conversation was stiff, and when the check came he tore the copy of the credit card receipt meticulously and creepily into smaller and smaller, equally neat pieces. When I declined to go out with him again he stalked me over the phone, hanging up each time I answered. I filed a police report to make him stop.

I missed Jeff and his calm, genuine presence. The scariest thing about him was that he'd want us to keep strictly kosher–how frightening was that, really? We wrote letters to each other each week, and despite the distance I felt we were growing closer. He wrote entertainingly about his week, his work, outings he took with friends; but they often turned sentimental, painting visions of our future in what I assumed could only mean marriage. Still, he remained maddeningly oblique. In one letter I thought he was proposing. Sort of. I read it again, and then again, looking for that proposal. Yes, there it was! Between the lines, subtle yet unmistakable. A vague proposal perhaps, or the mists of one to come. Oh, why didn't he just come out and say it? I wanted it to be a proposal. I called my mother and asked what she thought.

"If you have to ask, it's not a proposal," Mom said with her trademark blunt assessment. My parents liked Jeff, though Mom probably felt he was becoming "too religious." On the other hand, in my mid-twenties, my parents were ready to walk me down the aisle to a solid, responsible, kind man, even if it meant I would give up the right to bare arms and would be walking to shul on Saturdays, possibly pushing a double stroller. Better that than having me start husband hunting from scratch.

My hazy romantic visions cleared when Jeff visited me and was sporting a new accessory: a small red knitted kippah. I was startled. He had told me he was considering wearing it full-time, not just for Rabbi Lapin's classes or at shul. Now his public identity included this obvious marker that he was a religious Jewish man. I felt very self-conscious about his new look. I wondered what other people would think about him, about us. I was bothered that it bothered me, and understood it was my choice to embrace Jeff's decision and feel proud–or not.

Prepared with the next weapon in his arsenal, Jeff had brought me a book by Blu Greenberg, the most well-known of the Orthodox feminists, called *How to Run a Traditional Jewish Household*. He read me some passages that he hoped would prove to me that Orthodoxy could be compatible with feminism. He was now keeping Shabbos, and wanted me to share his vision of a life where one day a week we would protect the boundary between the sacred and the mundane, between work and personal space. I had not made any changes, Jewishly speaking, in Evanston. I was a frequent guest for Shabbos dinner at my friend Eileen and her family's home in nearby Skokie, which had a large Jewish population. I had met Eileen during a recent vacation I had taken in Israel, and when she learned that I was headed to Chicago for school, she opened her arms and her heart, calling me each week to make sure I had a place to go for Shabbos dinner, and a movie Saturday night with her and her other single girlfriends. We dubbed ourselves "The Skokie Girls," even though I was the import, and we gabbed a lot about just how much religious commitment we felt we could "tolerate" in husbands.

But my Saturdays had no Shabbos feel. I shopped a little at the farmer's market right on my street, studied in the library, met a friend for brunch. These were nice, quiet, and relaxing days. But I was just a student, with no one to care for other than myself. One day, I hoped to be married and a mother. What would my Saturdays look like then? What Jewish input would I be offering my children? Where would they find their sense of peoplehood, of purpose? It seemed the way of much of the Western world that without a religious commitment, middle class life could drift disproportionately onto materialistic concerns, or at least ignore spiritual concerns.

It hadn't occurred to me to carve out "sacred spaces" in my life, but it was starting to sound like a pretty good idea, perhaps like the idea of exercise sounds to a totally sedentary person. It may be more work than fun at first, but the enjoyment and rewards follow later. I had another realization, too. Jeff was very driven, a potential Type A personality who could easily become a workaholic. I didn't want to be married to a workaholic. I figured that if God Himself was drawing the line, saying, "Thou Shalt Not Work on Saturdays," I wouldn't have to.

I took Jeff to my favorite hangouts, including a poorly lit, musty, used bookstore heaving with literary delights. In one corner of the shop, we discovered a full set of Shakespeare's works in miniature, in green leather binding with gilt-edged pages, no more than an inch and a half high. We bought it–our first piece of community property, I thought happily. Marriage was surely only a few formalities away! But if not, I'd buy out his share. I wasn't giving up that Shakespeare collection for anything.

I also introduced Jeff to my friend and classmate Kathy, a devoted Catholic who attended mass at least once a week. I felt more of a kinship with Kathy than with most of the other students. Despite our different religions, she provided an understanding ear. When I shared some of my conflicts over Jewish religious commitment with her, she astonished me by saying, "I think Judaism is a great religion. If I weren't Catholic, I'd want to be Jewish."

Kathy said how much she respected Judaism's emphasis on family and community, and the stamp of morality and ethics it had given to civilization through the Old Testament. Earning Kathy's vote of confidence made an impact on me, especially after she told me about her exasperating argument with "Ron," a Jewish student. One night Kathy had tried to convince him that God exists.

"If God exists, let Him prove it to me," Ron demanded. "Let Him send some thunder or lightning right now and then I'd believe in Him!"

But when Kathy told me about this episode, I was embarrassed. I knew a lot of Jews like Ron, insisting on "proofs" in a way that was both childish and belligerent. Worse, I recognized that I had a little bit of Ron inside of me as well. I had also scoffed at traditions I did not understand. I had invested a lot of energy looking for reasons to judge Rabbi Lapin and his students because of their thirst for Jewish knowledge when I couldn't even name all the holidays on the calendar or the twelve tribes of Israel. Did I plan to ever outgrow my own stage of spiritual adolescence?

I didn't want to be like Ron or like my old college friend Patty. Meeting for coffee one afternoon, Patty arrived in a state of high dudgeon. That afternoon, a young Orthodox man had walked into the art gallery where she worked.

"Was he rude?" I asked.

"No, but whenever I see guys like that, wearing their kippahs and their tzitzit dangling from under their shirts, I think about how sexist Orthodoxy is, and it makes me so mad," she said.

Patty's visceral and extreme reaction shocked me. She was ready to convict a total stranger of sexism by association merely because he dressed like an Orthodox Jew. It was bigoted, and I was shaken by the realization that I also reacted to the sight of the Orthodox with instant negative associations. Yet I didn't know any Orthodox Jews personally. How did I know the stereotypes were true?

In one of our first journalism classes at Medill, an old-time professor taught us a maxim about looking for the truth in a story.

"If it walks like a duck, acts like a duck, and talks like a duck, it's a duck," he said. It was a funny and pithy lesson: don't overanalyze things. The truth might be right in front of you. As the year went by I accepted that my self-perception as a broad-minded liberal didn't match my behavior, which smacked–or maybe quacked–of intolerance. I decided to keep probing Judaism with the vigor and rigor that I tried to bring to any story I was covering, whether a court case, medical research, or societal trend. After all, weren't the stakes every bit as high?

Chapter 10

FRIENDSHIPS LOST AND FOUND

FALL 1986

WITH MY MASTER'S DEGREE IN HAND, I flew back to L.A. in high spirits, eager to be reunited with Jeff but admittedly getting impatient for him to propose. With increased exposure, the PJC community revealed itself as vibrant and even eclectic, with intelligent and mostly independent-minded people. There were a few folks who glommed onto the rabbi's every utterance as if it had thundered down directly from Mount Sinai. These people spoke almost exclusively about what the rabbi had most recently discussed, and Jeff and I planned to keep our distance from this depressing subculture of "Lapin lemmings."

But I had also calmed down enough so that I could allow myself to enjoy the Thursday night class. Rabbi Lapin had a remarkable intellect. It was impossible not to admire his vast knowledge, wit, and charismatic teaching style. Finally, I was learning substantial things about what the Torah said, and thereby more of Jewish history. I began to absorb the concept that we had a destiny that was still unfolding. My Hebrew reading and vocabulary were improving as well. If I worked hard enough, I, too, could achieve a baseline level of Jewish literacy.

Jeff and I became known as an established couple at PJC and were invited regularly for Shabbos meals by community members. I was struck by how socially integrated the community was, without boundaries of age, culture, or financial status. Most shul members were in their twenties and thirties, but the minority of couples in their fifties and sixties were every bit as popular as the younger set. In fact, Rabbi Lapin had explained that the word for community, *kahal,* was comprised of three letters (*kuf, hay*, and *lamed*) whose numerical values, respectively, were one hundred, five, and thirty. Those numbers represent past (the elderly), future (children) and present (people considered at full strength). The letter *lamed* (thirty) seems oddly placed at the end, when logically you'd think the core strength of the community would be sourced in young, yet mature adulthood. When I asked Rabbi Lapin about this, he was quick to answer.

"Without living links to the past and to the future, the present lacks vitality," he said. "The older people in the community more than pull their weight by reminding us all every day that without the past, much of our daily lives would lack meaning. The same goes for the little kids running around. The present tense in Hebrew almost doesn't exist. This teaches us to view the present not as a thinly sliced instant of time but as a process that seamlessly converts future into past."

This was another in an ongoing series of insights I loved to learn from the Hebrew language. Rabbi Lapin had said that a document with this level of sophistication and insight could not have been written by a human being.

Joe and Betty were one of the older couples in the community, and had only begun studying Torah when they were around sixty. Honestly, they were among the most remarkable people I had ever met. They were extraordinarily happy, as if they couldn't believe their good fortune at being part of this little band of *baalei teshuva* by the beach.

"Well, hello, come on in!" Joe invariably greeted guests at the door, stretching out the welcome in a melting, Southern drawl. His beard and oddly long haircut gave him an Amish look.

"Judy! Jeff! How nice to see you!" Betty would say, as if she hadn't seen us in six months when in fact she had seen us two days earlier, reaching out to give me a hug with a beatific smile. When I first met them, I was astounded: were these people for real? What's in that wine they're drinking Friday night? How can anyone be this unnaturally jovial all the time? Where's that quintessential Jewish edge, that faint shudder of anxiety just below the surface? I expected people in their sixties to have a few complaints about growing infirmities, their conversation tinged with a bit of cynicism at the harder things that life had dished out. Joe and Betty would have none of that. They were grateful for everything, even Betty's bouts with skin cancer.

"Joe took care of me and changed my bandages every day, and we became closer, even after forty years of marriage," Betty told me. "My face was heavily bandaged, so I couldn't read like I normally do, and all I could do was listen to Torah tapes. Listening to those tapes made me feel I was growing through my suffering. I was sure the cancer was a sort of decree helping me make up for my shortcomings, so I was happy."

If Disneyland ever needed Orthodox Jewish grandparents as mascots, Joe and Betty would have fit the bill: they were the happiest couple on Earth. With Joe wearing his kippah full-time, attending the minyan every day, and Betty wearing a silvery wig and long sleeves, you'd hardly have guessed that they had belonged to Reform or Conservative synagogues for nearly all their years of marriage. Joe was a fifth-generation Reform Jew who hadn't even known what a kippah was for. But when Betty accepted an invitation to hear an Orthodox speaker in a private home, she was inspired enough to try to convince "my sweet husband Joe" to start learning more. Within a few years, they were committed enough to move from their home in northern Santa Monica into a home on Rose Avenue in Venice, down the block from the Lapins and a mile's walk to the shul along the beach.

Betty told me that when she and Joe did decide to make their kitchen kosher, keep Shabbos, and attend Rabbi Lapin's classes regularly, one of her close friends said to her, "We've lost you."

"This friend had grown up observant and then became Conservative," Betty said. "I protested that no, she hadn't lost us, we could still have dinner together at a kosher restaurant and still be friends, but unfortunately our bond did not last. Even though we couldn't keep those old friendships, HaShem has given us so many new wonderful friends, especially young friends like you!"

It would have been easy to scorn their relentless good cheer as the product of naïveté or having had a little too much of that old-time religion. Joe and Betty's faith was pure and simple, but they were not simple or naïve people. Joe was a civil engineer and had served as a Navy officer in World War II. Betty had been a schoolteacher, and together they had raised their son and daughter in the social maelstrom of the 1960s. Joe and Betty did an extreme renovation of their interior lives at a point past midlife, pursuing what they saw as a better course, even at the cost of decades-old friendships and the disbelief of their daughter. Their son had already become Shabbos-observant.

I could never be as "blissed out" as Betty or share her indefatigable happiness, but I fell in love with her and Joe. Their joy in life was real and infectious. They proved that you could grow older physically while staying young and agile both spiritually and psychologically. Their affection and respect for each other were profound, and it was clear they were beloved role models for almost everyone else in the community. Their marriage reinforced my hope that if I married Jeff, we would also continue to grow in love, devotion, and depth, our union never getting stale.

One time at a wedding reception I was chatting with Betty. She saw Joe across the room, where he was talking with another man. Gazing at him with adoration she said, "Every time Joe walks into the room, I still see that handsome Navy officer I first met more than forty-five years ago." Betty had this way of leaving you speechless.

Joe and Betty's serenity and pleasure in life, and their popularity among "the younger set" reinforced a few of Rabbi Lapin's claims that I had questioned at first. One was that in a Torah community, it should be natural for all ages of adults to mix socially, because of the shared value system running through the generations as well as the element of respect among the young for elders. I also saw, to my surprise and somewhat to my chagrin, that Joe and Betty were not exactly outliers in their contentment. The other couples who had become *baalei teshuva* in midlife also expressed a similar joyful energy, undimmed by life's travails. They had that *joie de vivre* that I had seen in Cece and Papa, along with the religious faith of my Nana and Papa, but without that *oy de vivre* that I was afraid would come with the package. Here in Venice, I saw the potential for a life of intellectual and even cultural sophistication, along with deep Jewish faith and knowledge.

I had not known where to find this or even that it existed.

But understanding what the Torah said required going well beneath the surface, which you could only do with an experienced guide. Without digging deeper, you could easily scoff at the idea that the Torah was actually *progressive*. But more than two thousand years before Magna Carta, the Torah had introduced sweeping concepts of individual rights: property rights; rule of law for everyone, including the servant class; literacy for everyone, not just the ruling classes; accountability under the law. These were radical concepts in the ancient world. Sure, God expected allegiance to His laws, and there were heavy-duty side effects (drought, infertility, early death, etc.) if instead you chose to "do your own thing," as the poster in my childhood bedroom advised. This was tough love all right.

But this path was also sounding like something that could help ease many of the ills of society. As I saw it, modern values were increasingly fungible. Divorce rates were rising and too many children suffered the effects from sadly fractured families. More and more books, movies, and popular songs were breathtakingly negative, coarse, violent, and hypersexualized. How could I protect my future children from all this? How could I preserve the innocence that should have remained rightfully theirs for a few more years? I wasn't a prude, but I also felt the bottom was falling out of society's moral and ethical standards. Looking at magazine covers at the supermarket checkout, I saw more feature articles with teaser headlines like, "8 Signs You're in an Abusive Relationship," or, "How to Cope when He's Drinking Again." Were these problems so pervasive? I know it's easy to romanticize the past, and every generation enjoyed progress in some areas, but morally I felt we were going backward.

Of course, there was no such thing as a total inoculation against any and all forms of social pathology. Even Jews who kept kosher and observed Shabbos could have emotional problems, marital discord, or addictions. But I believed that given a baseline of emotional health, living "the Torah way" could add depth and happiness, as well as a sense of purpose and identity, and that living in a community of like-minded people could offer some degree of shelter against some of these problems. And when problems did arise, Jews usually had your backs. Jewish communities were famous throughout history for offering dignified communal support in times of need.

I became increasingly willing to place my bet on Rabbi Lapin's philosophy of living a life of "rules, rituals, and restraints." I didn't want to go through life being concussed by the rapidly changing philosophies that passed for wisdom in the broader culture. Meanwhile, the Torah had been a constant value and belief system for more than three thousand years. Jews had also lasted more than three thousand years, despite all efforts to get rid of us. Maybe there was a connection.

I would never understand all of God's laws or ways. I might never grow to like all of them, either. But not understanding or liking them all didn't negate their truth; it only affirmed the limitations of human insight.

It was still an intimidating and slightly scary choice to live with the stringencies of Torah values. It meant I'd have to adjust the way I ate, dressed, spoke, and even thought, to align myself with what I now understood was right. Many of these things would feel like sacrifices. If and when some of my longstanding friendships did fade away, I would miss them and feel nostalgic for the good memories we shared. But it often happened to people after college anyway, even without the additional ingredient of religious observance. And if I did lose a few, I still had already gained some new friends around my age through PJC. And of course, I had Betty and Joe!

The diversity in the PJC community was helpful in reassuring me that my transition to a more religious lifestyle was a good idea. People who drove to shul on Shabbos were equally welcomed both in the synagogue and as guests in people's homes. Rabbi Lapin was proud of this diversity in religious observance as a measure of the community's success.

"If the day ever comes when everyone is walking to shul and no one is driving, we will have failed in our mission," he said. I agreed.

I had anticipated a great deal of conformity and initially fretted that the women of PJC would strike me as Jewish "Stepford Wives," all bewigged and consumed with trading recipes when they weren't changing diapers. Yet few of the women I met had matched my unfair and unkind stereotypes. Nearly all were high achievers, many with advanced degrees in law, business, psychology, social work, or education. There were several writers in the bunch, men and women. Some mothers worked part-time or full-time, though the majority had parked their careers for the time being in favor of full-time motherhood. And if your clan already had three, four, or five kids and was still growing, motherhood was more than a full-time job.

In truth, I was hardly a feminist firebrand myself. I wanted to become a wife and mother every bit as much as I wanted a successful writing career. In college, I couldn't admit how much I wanted this because marriage and motherhood had been deemed a second-rate career by *avant-garde* thinkers and many in the professoriate. In my new circles at PJC, I could safely share my hidden resentment of that message. And now that I had weekly exposure to young mothers and their lively broods, I became humbled by the stakes involved in nurturing emotionally healthy children. Yes, I would absolutely trade some professional advancement for the privilege of being a home-based mom and knowing I gave my all to what I had furtively considered the most important job in the world. The media were hyping the idea that women could "have it all," both committed motherhood and a fully satisfying career. That struck me as naïve and false.

Jeff and I took a major step and asked to be hosted overnight with PJC families on Friday nights so that we could keep a more "authentic" Shabbos that didn't violate halacha, Jewish law. I was hosted by David and Sharon, who had three young children. They made me feel comfortable right away in their ranch-style, four-bedroom home. They were friendly, down-to-earth, and open. David was playing classical music in his office, a room with double glass doors adjacent to the living room, where the two eldest children, five-year-old Devorah and three-year-old Eli, were playing. I liked the music but was unfamiliar with it. I asked David what it was.

"It's Mahler's 4th Symphony," he explained with the enthusiasm of a passionate music lover. "I actually think that the third movement of the symphony is more in the category of 'miracle' rather than just 'great music.'" I knew nothing about classical music, and beyond being able to identify the famous first four notes of Beethoven's 5th Symphony, I was a blank slate. We listened to the piece for a few minutes and then David paused the music.

"You can hear that this music is mostly melancholy and even lonely, but it's about to get frisky and happy. See if you can hear the 'pulse' in the bass strings. It's plunking in the background constantly."

I listened, watching David as he listened to the music. He was completely engrossed, absorbing every note. He knew so much about music and was so passionate about it that I was surprised to learn he owned a preschool and was not involved professionally in the music world himself. It was easy even for me to catch the "frisky and happy" transition in the movement, but I admitted I could not catch the undercurrent of the plunking bass. David had what seemed to me an astounding collection of classical music, from Beethoven to Wagner (even though Wagner was an anti-Semite), including multiple recordings of the same works. I had come to Sharon and David to observe my first Shabbos fully and was unexpectedly getting a music appreciation lesson as a bonus. I decided not to tell David that my "classical" music favorites didn't go back earlier than the 1960s and the Beatles, or that I had been blasting Bruce Springsteen in the car on the way over to his house. I didn't expect to become a Mahler fan, at least not based on his 4th Symphony, but I was happy to register more evidence that becoming Torah-observant didn't mean you had to check your secular cultural interests at the door.

As the time to light Shabbos candles drew near, I watched Sharon in action and tried to imagine myself in her shoes: She was a multitasking maven, stirring sauces, sautéing vegetables, crossing off tasks from her Friday to-do list one by one. She occasionally cooed at her baby in the high chair, who was leisurely eating Cheerios and alternately stuffing them under the vinyl seat. She brokered a truce between her two older children; fielded an urgent call with a request to host a last-minute dinner guest; and monitored the housekeeper (who was herself monitoring children in the bath) and setting the table for guests, all while trying to make newcomers like me feel at home. I felt a little dizzy amid the torrent of activity.

"Sorry for the chaos," she smiled apologetically as a half-naked preschooler still dripping from the bath darted through the kitchen. Managing a traditional Jewish household, I saw, was intimidating. It took a great deal of skill, patience, fortitude, humor, and wisdom, especially with several little kids underfoot.

Before giving her children snacks, Sharon prompted them to make a *bracha*, or blessing, over the food. I knew the *hamotzei* blessing before eating bread and the *borei pri hagafen* blessing before wine, but I did not know there were several other blessings for different categories of foods: one for fruits that grew from trees; another for produce picked from the earth; one for baked goods such as cookies or pretzels; yet another one for drinks, meat, or fish.

"*Baruch Ata Ado-nai, Elo-heynu Melech HaOlam, borei menei mezonot*," Devorah said, her expression solemn, before sinking her little teeth into a cookie. I felt annoyed. "Can't a little kid just enjoy her cookie without thanking God?" I thought. "How regimented are these people's lives?" But my annoyance was fleeting. My next thought, almost instantaneous, was that it was actually brilliant to train young children to stop and consider where their food came from, to acknowledge it as a gift before chowing down. I could see that the laws of keeping kosher, including making blessings before and after eating and waiting a few hours after eating a meat meal before having any dairy products, also instilled self-discipline and appreciation. You can't always eat what you want–a lesson I had yet to master myself. I picked up a small booklet from Sharon's breakfast table containing all the before- and after-blessings and decided to try to learn them for myself. Who wants to be shown up in the *bracha* department by a five-year-old?

I quickly became a "frequent flier" Shabbos guest with David and Sharon, feeling a little less like a stranger in a strange land. I loved their children, read to them, and played with them when they lacked more exciting, shorter company. Still, I clung to a prickly pride in my ambivalence about living as religiously as David and Sharon and many other PJC couples did. One Shabbos morning I was having coffee with Sharon and one of her neighbors, Deborah, in the kitchen. I listened as Sharon and Deborah discussed amusing and exasperating situations they had experienced with their children during the past week. As they described the tussles, tantrums, and timeouts (a few of which were for the mommies) I wondered how I would have handled similar situations. I was glad to listen to them, because they sounded wise and practical, and I was filing away what I heard in my brain, hoping I would remember their parenting smarts when I had my own young'uns.

Eventually, the conversation turned to hair-covering, my "magnificent obsession." Both Sharon and Deborah kept their hair strictly under wraps. I had told Jeff that I would never cover my hair after we were married. Ever.

"Fine," he had said. "I won't ever ask you to. I know you need to go at your own pace." His reassurance didn't entirely satisfy me. I didn't doubt his word, but would I feel like a rebel if we lived in this community and I never adopted this mitzvah? Would I feel an unspoken pressure to conform? I wondered how some of the other women who didn't cover their hair felt about it. Anyhow, I didn't know any of them well enough to ask.

"I'd hate to have to keep my hair covered up all the time," I confessed. "I can't imagine doing it. And I think it would feel very fake if I wore a wig."

"Whenever anyone asks me if this is my own hair, I say, 'Of course it's mine. I paid for it!'" laughed Deborah. I was disarmed by Deborah's sense of humor, quick-witted and self-deprecating. Both she and Sharon easily saw the humor and irony in their lives.

"Look, this is a difficult mitzvah for a lot of women," Sharon warned. "The issues you have with Orthodoxy regarding men's and women's roles won't go away by themselves. Your concerns are very real and you need to explore them thoroughly. You don't want to commit to something if your heart isn't in it."

I appreciated Sharon's straight talk. No one was trying to convince me that theirs was the "right" way to live. One of the things I liked about Sharon, Deborah and a few other of my new friends was that they respected the difficulty of the decisions I needed to make. After all, *they* had made these decisions, too. Who was I to question how much struggle they may have gone through in the process?

"I really do like what I see in your families," I said, sipping my coffee and hoping there was enough hot water left in the urn for me to have a second cup. "There's a wholesomeness about your lives that I want very much for myself. It just seems to come with a package of extras I hadn't anticipated."

"Oh yeah, wholesome is our middle name," joked Deborah, whose beautiful artwork and calligraphy graced the homes of many couples in the community. "You and Jeff are individuals, and always will be. Hopefully, the two of you will find a way that works for you both and keeps you here in Venice. We like you guys."

I liked Deborah and Sharon also. I liked the way they lived–at least, most of it. Would these new friendships be enough to help me go the distance?

Chapter 11

DECISION TIME

1986–1987

JEFF FREQUENTLY SAID THAT HE UNDERSTOOD and accepted my need to progress at my own pace. In reality, he had a short list of non-negotiable issues related to Jewish observance. If we married and moved into this community, he wanted us to observe Shabbos and kashrut at the same level as Rabbi Lapin defined their observances. I was ready to take on those two and made a mental note to stop in for the eggplant parmesan at one of my favorite non-kosher restaurants a few more times before I had to say *arrivaderci*, Maria.

The third non-negotiable on the list was much tougher: strictly following the laws of t*aharat hamishpacha,* or "family purity." When I learned what those laws were about, I was not happy. These laws mandate that from the beginning of a woman's menstrual period and for seven days afterward until she immerses in the *mikveh* (a ritual bath), married couples do not touch one another, not even holding hands. I mean *gornisht*, nada, zip. After the woman's immersion in the mikveh, she is considered to be in a state of newness and spiritual purity, and only then does the couple resume their physical intimacy. A weeklong "timeout" made sense to me, as I thought about the old adage, "familiarity breeds contempt." But a minimum of twelve days? That sounded extreme. It sounded *Orthodox.*

I protested, "You see? The Torah considers women to be 'dirtied' by our menses. Otherwise, why would we need to go to a ritual bath? That's so offensive and wrong," I complained.

"Not true," Jeff said. "The Torah considers sex between married couples to be sacred. It encourages it and celebrates it, but with appropriate boundaries. Like everything else, it needs a framework to help a couple keep their relationship on a high level. Women immerse in the mikveh to cleanse a 'spiritual impurity.' That's not a slam against women. This is about something more subtle and sensitive. The egg that was not fertilized that month represents the loss of a potential human life. Blood represents the absence of purity in the same way that darkness represents an absence of light."

Naturally, Jeff had been reading about all this from well-known books I had seen on the bookshelves in many PJC homes, including *Waters of Eden* by Aryeh Kaplan and *The Secret of Jewish Femininity* by Tehilla Abramov. Not having read any of this material or discussed it with anyone truly knowledgeable, I was armed only with the myths and prejudice against the practice of mikveh I had heard growing up. Listening to Jeff, I was reminded of the slogan I had once seen on a T-shirt that said, "You can't have a battle of wits with someone who is unarmed."

"Besides," Jeff said, "men have spiritual impurities, too, and go to the mikveh. All converts go as part of their conversion ceremony. And when the Temple stood in Jerusalem thousands of years ago, the *kohen gadol* (high priest) immersed in a mikveh before performing the Temple service. A lot of men go before holidays or before Shabbos. I plan to go on our wedding day. This is not about a physical flaw. It's about the immersion of the soul."

Oh boy, I thought. Talk about deep waters! I was glad to know

Judaism considered sex between married couples holy. I knew it was a wise religion! And I was pleased, albeit grudgingly, that men also went to the ritual bath. I focused on absorbing the new idea that going to the mikveh bath didn't mean I needed "fixing" because I'm a woman.

"I need more time to consider what this will mean for us and whether I can accept it," I said. "A two-week break still seems extreme, even if the philosophy is not what I thought it was. This will affect us much more than not eating out in non-kosher restaurants anymore, or not shopping on Saturdays."

"I know. But this will help us keep this aspect of our marriage special and exciting," he said. "We may not always have physical intimacy, but we can always have emotional intimacy, even during the 'timeout' weeks."

"But if we argue, we can't kiss and make up," I said.

"We won't argue," he said, smiling. "But if we do, we'll have to make up through everything else we have: our words, our expressions, our tone of voice, writing each other notes. There are many non-physical ways of relating. It could also be a barometer of how well we relate to each other overall."

I thought about Nana Cohen. Had she ever gone to the mikveh, or had she left that custom back in Kiev? It was frustrating to have discovered my curiosity too late to find out.

Around that time I was working as a copy editor at the *Los Angeles Jewish Journal,* a weekly newspaper. It was the perfect job for me, bringing me face to face–literally–with a wide spectrum of Jewish ideas. The *Journal* had rotating columnists whose viewpoints ranged from the staunchly secular and liberal to consistently conservative voices, including those of Dennis Prager, Michael Medved, and Dr. Diane Medved, whose positions on politics, culture, and sometimes Judaism were usually to the right of my own. I hunkered down over the copy, focusing on the flow of the text, grammar and punctuation.

To my surprise, once I began focusing closely on each argument, I found that the traditional voices often resonated with me more than I would have guessed. The left-of-center columnists wrote tirelessly and, to my mind, tiresomely about feminism and inequality, viewing everything through that prism. Was everything related somehow to sexism and social injustice? I didn't think so. I felt an undercurrent of anger also suffused their writings.

My exposure to a Torah-based community and to Orthodox perspectives had been limited to what I had observed in Rabbi Lapin's Venice community. Still, based on my experiences and observations, I felt that some of these liberal voices unfairly convicted the Torah as anti-woman. I saw educated women who had compared the secular lives they knew firsthand with the much more traditional religious life of Torah observance, and found the promise and potential of the latter more appealing. They were highly respected, and they seemed happy. They couldn't *all* be faking it. The few snippets of Torah I had learned or heard about already that dealt with women also showed the Torah had much more respect for women's wisdom, along with their influence and wishes, than what I had expected.

For example, in Genesis, when the matriarch Sarah tells Avraham to eject his second wife, Hagar, along with their son Ishmael, Avraham is grieved. Ishmael is Avraham's firstborn son, but Sarah believes that the boy's mocking ways toward Isaac pose a potentially dire threat to their son. God instructs Avraham to listen to Sarah because she is correct, and consoles Avraham by promising that both Isaac and Ishmael will be progenitors of great nations. Only then does Avraham reluctantly send them away. Some commentators cite this episode as proof that Sarah was gifted with a higher level of prophecy than Avraham. In the Book of Samuel, Hannah, who also suffered from infertility, is misjudged by the priest Eli as praying while drunk. In truth, she was tearfully praying for the gift of a child, a son she could dedicate to the service of God. Hannah defends herself and explains her actions to Eli, and the priest blesses her that her prayer will come true. That son became Samuel the prophet.

Hannah's soulful, nearly inaudible articulation of prayer established the model for how Jews have prayed throughout the generations–moving their lips and pronouncing the words. There is also Rebecca's famous scheme to get her husband, Isaac, to give the blessing of the firstborn to Jacob instead of to the elder twin, Esau. Despite her fudging the truth, her actions are considered correct. And when the daughters of a man named Tzelafchad complained about a lack of women's property rights in the land of Israel because they were unmarried, Moses took their complaint directly to God, and the Almighty ruled with the daughters.

It's not that the Torah claims to be egalitarian. It doesn't. It isn't. But it was hardly turning out to be the nasty anti-woman treatise that liberal conventional wisdom had made it out to be.

The more I was learning from Rabbi Lapin, the more humbled I began to feel at my own previous rush to judgment about Jewish traditions and teaching. I was even feeling a little defensive on behalf of Orthodoxy when I encountered this anti-religious bias in the columns I edited that were written by people who lacked the educational chops to make these judgments.

In contrast, the conservative columnists often tapped into the larger truths about human psychology, Jewish spirituality, and history. They pointed out lessons and values from history that they said must help guide us toward decisions on the future. This also made sense to me.

I was also becoming seriously annoyed by the derisive comments I heard from the Jewish staffers in the office about the Orthodox community. They shot off mean-spirited remarks about the Orthodox community many times and even disparaged essays submitted by a regular contributor who was Orthodox. This is the *Jewish Journal*, I said to myself. Why was there so little respect for core Jewish values in a publication dedicated to reporting on Jewish issues?

Ironically, Carol, the Catholic senior copy editor, had much more respect for Judaism than much of the Jewish staff, and she was also mystified at this dismissive attitude of some staffers toward their coreligionists. It was a happy coincidence that I ended up working with Carol. On my first day at the job, I realized that she had been the editor who purchased the first humor essay I had sold to the *Los Angeles Herald Examiner*, my first byline in a big city newspaper. Carol and I often talked about life, marriage, faith, and how I could square my feminist ideals with Orthodoxy. As my friend Kathy had done in Evanston, Carol encouraged me to continue exploring my religious heritage. She considered herself a feminist but didn't see any contradiction between being a career woman who planned to put family first. I thought: how crazy is it that I am collecting Catholic friends who encourage my Jewish religious growth, while the secular Jews in my midst seem mostly cynical about all things Orthodox?

And yet I couldn't shake my insecurities that Jeff's vision of living what he called an "authentic" Jewish life might be more than I could handle. In a Torah life, Jeff had found his "true north." I was trying to make it my own, but could I go the distance and be true to myself? I couldn't bear to hold him back from living the way he wanted to, needed to, and deserved to. Over the next several weeks, my internal conflict reached a breaking point. It hadn't helped that we had recently accepted an invitation to a Shabbos dinner with one of the "Lapin lemmings," a guy who sort of gave me the creeps. In his dimly lit apartment, with a series of clocks on the wall showing different times around the world, all anyone talked about was what Rabbi Lapin had discussed that evening. I felt disoriented and, for the first time in my life, claustrophobic. My heart was racing and I had trouble breathing. I turned to Jeff and whispered, "Let's get out of here." We left right away, and Jeff apologized profusely. He was upset by the evening as well.

Someone we knew who worked in Jewish outreach had quipped, "You have to be 'you-ish' to be Jewish." It was a cute yet profound line. It argued against the tendency of "converts" (even if they were already Jewish) to follow a cookie cutter uniformity in their thinking and practice. This was one of my biggest fears, even though the uniformity, while very distressing, was still more the exception than the rule. I *wanted* to want a Torah-observant life. There was so much in it that I saw was good and beautiful and wholesome and true. My Cohen genes urged me on, but my stubborn Rosenfeld independent streak would not be quieted.

I felt I was experiencing that same kind of panic that Jeff had felt during his third week at Aish HaTorah in Jerusalem, when the weight of all the new ideas about God, history, and life's purpose became overwhelming, causing him to pack up and leave and continue growing at his own pace. Now, after a nearly two-year courtship, despite our natural chemistry, our shared outlook on so many of life's situations, a kindred sense of the absurd, and all the work we had done so far to reach a shared direction for our future, I was scared. Was I trying to convince myself of something that might never feel absolutely genuine? Over the course of several days, the feeling grew into a gut-wrenching heartsickness. I had to speak up.

My heart pounding, my mouth dry as sawdust, I said, "I've thought about this over and over. And I've tried to see myself as the kind of wife I know you want. But I'm not sure I'm that person. I love you, and you have been very patient, but I'm still too conflicted about the religious aspect. I can't hold you back. You deserve someone who wants the same thing you want."

"What are you saying?" he asked, his voice barely above a whisper.

"I think . . . I think we need to break up."

Chapter 12

THE PLUNGE

OCTOBER 1986

AFTER A MISERABLE AND SLEEPLESS NIGHT, I was roused from my brief, troubled sleep by the phone ringing early in the morning.

"I'm coming over," Jeff said, his voice haggard and hoarse. "We are not breaking up." All I could feel was relief. I had thought I was being responsible, honest, and fair by cutting loose from the relationship. I hoped I would feel a burden had lifted, but instead I felt the weight of a sickening sorrow.

Within thirty minutes he had arrived at my parents' home in the West San Fernando Valley, where I had been living since returning from Evanston. We embraced and cried.

"You are more important to me than any shul, any rabbi, or any community," he said. "We don't have to live in the Venice community. We'll live wherever you want." I couldn't ask for more than that. We spent the day together, slowly recovering from the short-lived trauma that I had inflicted on us both. We would immediately start shopping around for other possible shuls and communities where we would start our lives together.

Rabbi Lapin's Shul on the Beach and community was an outlier in Los Angeles, the only Orthodox group in the Santa Monica-Venice area with more than a handful of members. But only six miles east, the Pico-Robertson neighborhood where I had lived previously was burgeoning with the newly observant. There were at least a dozen Orthodox synagogues of every flavor "in the 'hood," as people liked to call it. Aside from the larger, established Ashkenazi type of synagogue that drew people with European roots and customs, there were a growing number of smaller shuls catering to Jewish immigrants from Iran, Iraq, Morocco, France, Egypt, Syria, and even Yemen, whose Middle Eastern melodies, rituals and style of service would remind them of home. Along Pico Boulevard there were pizza shops, upscale restaurants, bustling bakeries, Judaica stores, day schools, a mikveh, and every other amenity that a kosher- and Shabbos-observant Jew could want.

Jeff and I looked at some apartments in this neighborhood and tried out various shuls on Shabbos. In short order, we rejected them all. One drab little place had an offensive, Berlin Wall-style *mechitza* that divided the men's and women's sections by a floor-to-ceiling curtain–women in the back. I was so incensed at the thoughtlessness of this setup, which cut women off both visually and, I felt, emotionally, that we left after ten minutes. I don't think I would have stayed if Moses himself had been the guest speaker.

At a much larger, nicer and more affluent congregation, the women sat as per tradition in a raised tier of the synagogue above the men's section, with excellent visibility, but the crowd talked incessantly through the service. We didn't like this either and agreed this showed an insensitivity of an entirely different type. It was a shame: the rabbi was an outstanding speaker and the people mostly friendly. We managed to find fault with one after another shul: uninspired by the rabbi, not made to feel welcome enough, or the vibe just wasn't right.

Seeing the competition made PJC's Shul on the Beach rise in my estimation. In Venice, the seating was separate but equal, with the *mechitza* straight down the middle of the synagogue and not too high. Men and women had equal visual access to the main action on the *bimah*, or podium, where the Torah was read. And after visiting the chatty shul, I realized how much I appreciated the decorum at PJC. Yeah, Jews love to talk, and one friend of ours defended the yakkity Yids, saying he felt it made the place feel more "vibrant." But Jeff and I found it just plain rude. Besides, I had a long, long way to go before I could come close to understanding the depth of the Hebrew prayers. Rabbi Lapin's lessons showed me each week how nearly every word in Hebrew had nuanced meanings. That meant that until I could understand what each word meant, I was missing out on the meaning of the prayers. I was in shul to try to talk to God and to try to hear Him, too. This was still very new to me, and I wanted to get it right. It would take years for me to learn to pray with sincerity and understanding. I wouldn't be able to do so in an overly schmoozy shul.

Remarkably, after all we had been through, Jeff still hadn't remembered to actually ask me to marry him. I had a hard time understanding this oversight and decided I would need to clear my throat and suggest that he get on with it. A few weeks later, on New Year's Day, we took a walk in Marina del Rey, enjoying the late afternoon sunshine, and he asked me to sit down on a bench overlooking the marina. As I sat, he remained standing, reached into his pocket, knelt down on one knee, and presented me with . . . a handwritten note on blue stationery embossed with his name, Jeffrey A. Gruen. On the front flap of the note he wrote, "Will you please . . ." and as I opened the note my heart thudded powerfully even as I knew the next words: ". . . Marry me?"

Of course, I said yes, all the while wondering, *I thought you were going to pull a ring out of your pocket! Where's my ring? My blingy, shiny, I've-been-waiting-for-this-for-two-and-a-half years ring?* (Watching so many romantic movies growing up had not done me any favors. In real life sometimes you have to wait for the ring.) I felt happy yet also somehow stunned that, finally, we would begin to plan a wedding and our life together. We went out to dinner to celebrate, but Jeff appeared nervous, ordering a second beer and mumbling *sotto voce*, "I know this will all work out. I know it will!"

I, a teetotaler, sat there watching a lifetime of engagement scenario fantasies go down in a foamy head of Heineken. Fighting off feelings of hurt, I channeled my mother. Mom always seemed to know how to handle tricky situations. Waiting for our pasta dinners, I decided that Mom would quietly let him deal with his nerves. This may not have been the engagement evening of my dreams, but I believed in us. If Jeff needed a bit of alcoholic lubrication to adjust to the idea that we were going to be married, I would wait it out. And if he didn't get over it quickly, I'd start drinking too.

Fortunately, he had recovered his equanimity by the next day, and we immediately met with Michael Medved, president of the PJC community, and asked him for any leads on apartments near the shul. Michael happened to own a two-bedroom condo that he was happy to sell to us. We were thrilled with the opportunity. A few weeks later, Michael announced our engagement on *Shabbos* at the end of the service, with our parents in attendance. I was overwhelmed at the shouts of "Mazal tov!" and the singing and clapping that heralded the news. I knew that Jews love weddings, but I hadn't known that Orthodox Jews really, really were wild for them.

I was taken aback when one man came up to me outside the shul after the service and said, "I cannot wait to dance at your wedding! I simply cannot wait!" This man was socially awkward, single, and not a friend of ours. It hadn't occurred to me to include him on our invite list. But in that instant, I realized that we needed to invite him and that this was really what of being part of a community is about: including people in your lives whom you might not find the most congenial or comfortable. The mitzvah of welcoming guests, to one's home or a wedding, meant not just thinking about your favorite people, but specifically those who might otherwise be left out.

In no time flat, we caught some flak for our plans for an Orthodox wedding, especially as we slowly introduced our families to some concepts and practices they had never dreamed of for their children's weddings. One of them was no mixed dancing at the reception.

When my Aunt Eleanor heard this during one Friday night dinner, she burst out, "Do you mean to tell me I can't dance with my husband at your wedding?" Her eyes were set in a steely challenge. I felt ill-prepared to answer her. After all, I had committed to the "package deal" of Jewish observance, so I could hardly tell my fun yet feisty Aunt Eleanor that I agreed that the separate dancing for men and women at the wedding smacked of religious fundamentalism.

"Yes, that's what we mean, but only at our wedding. You can dance with Hal as much as you like before or after the wedding," Jeff dove in to rescue me. Hal was Aunt Eleanor's third husband, so she had a lot of experience with wedding receptions.

"Besides," I offered, eager to add something as a junior member of the defense bar, "when women dance together in groups and men dance together in groups, nobody is left out because they don't have a partner. Think of all the single people who won't have to wait for someone to ask them to dance." I couldn't help but remember my stinging loneliness at the wedding I had attended with the Doc where he danced with seemingly every young woman there other than me.

"Well, that part's true," Aunt Eleanor admitted.

Weddings were in the air in Venice that year. In a congregation of about one hundred and fifty people, the steady stream of wedding invitations was set to significantly boost the married census. The timing for us was superb because Jeff had only been to one Orthodox wedding before, and I hadn't been to any. At the weddings that preceded ours, we were both overwhelmed by the almost convulsive joy unleashed on the dance floor, the uproarious gags and skits, and the songs and revelry, all performed to entertain the bride and groom. The lively antics were so much fun that my concern over a lack of couples dancing faded quickly.

Orthodox Jews take the mitzvah of entertaining the bride and the groom very seriously, unleashing their inner kosher party animal. At the weddings we attended, against the auditory backdrop of the band playing Hebrew dances and klezmer music, we watched men perform handstands, cartwheels, and the Russian *kazatzka* dance. One rode onto the dance floor on his unicycle; another set his hat on fire and danced his way in front of the bride and groom with the flaming fedora on his head. Quick wardrobe changes transferred a trio of men from their formal suits into wetsuits with surfboards (for a groom who surfed); at a wedding right before Hanukkah, one guest emerged on the dance floor in a blue and white Santa suit.

Not to be outdone, women danced as feverishly as the men, sometimes in costumes, often with funny hats, waving batons, blowing whistles to help "manage" the traffic on the dance floor, jumping rope, dancing with Hula-Hoops, shaking maracas, and pulling an array of other party props out of a literal bag of tricks. Even Rabbi Lapin, whose staid British manner kept him mostly a spectator on the dance floor, put on a Sherlock Holmes-esque trench coat and did a three-legged walking trick with a deadpan expression on his face. At one point when the dancing and music were at a high pitch, bride and groom were hoisted high up on chairs by sturdy friends, each holding one end of a handkerchief and "dancing" together in the air. As their chairs dipped and teetered dangerously to one side, some brides held onto their seats, appearing momentarily terror-struck. The grooms just grinned like rugged oarsmen on class 4 rapids, blithely unconcerned over any risk of taking a tumble. Jeff and I loved adding our energy to these weddings, to have a chance to join in the uproarious festivities.

"There's nothing like an Orthodox wedding," our friend Alan observed when we were reliving the highlights of a recent celebration. "The happiness is a lot more than that one man and one woman merging their lives, it's about the entire Jewish world becoming stronger by this new union."

In the wedding ceremony, in fact, the couple is said to be creating a *bayis ne'eman*, or "faithful house" of Israel. When your nation is as numerically tiny as the people of Israel, each and every single new household counts.

There were a few other conflicts in addition to the griping about the segregated dancing. Mom had her heart set on ordering a cake from a popular bakery, but when we discovered that their kosher status was not an acceptable level for the hotel where we had signed a contract, Mom balked. She wanted a cake from that bakery for her daughter's wedding. She saw nothing wrong with the kosher status of the bakery. What could be in there, lard? But the standards to keep the kosher status of a hotel's kosher kitchen were very strict.

Many foods that seemed so innocent still required a kosher *hechsher*, or supervisory stamp of approval–even cakes. For instance, food dyes could contain pigments that came from insect carcasses. Aside from the gross-out quality of that source, no insect or insect derivative can be kosher. Also, many kinds of margarine include traces of dairy that would render a "dairy" status to the entire cake, unacceptable after a meat meal. When I learned these unappetizing facts, it helped me understand why the rules had to be so strict, and there was no arguing with the catering manager at the hotel. Unhappily, Mom defaulted to another bakery whose kosher status had never been questioned.

A much more worrisome conflict arose over who would preside over the ceremony. Mom wanted Rabbi Wise, the emeritus rabbi of our Conservative synagogue, to officiate along with Rabbi Lapin. Rabbi Wise was a kind and good man and had been a family friend for more than forty years. When Jeff and I met with Rabbi Lapin about plans for the wedding, I relayed my mother's request. He frowned.

"I'm afraid that will be impossible," he said. "You have to understand that according to my principles and for my reputation, I cannot co-officiate with a rabbi from a branch of Judaism that I believe has damaged the integrity of halacha."

"This will cause a huge problem for us," I said, alarmed. "My mother will never accept this. And it seems unfair to me as well." I didn't want to give Mom more reasons to paint Orthodoxy as inflexible, which it was, at least in this case. She deserved to have some things go her way, too!

"Of course I do want your mother to be happy," he continued, "so let me think about what we can do."

I knew Rabbi Lapin would not budge, but Jeff and I had been assured by other congregation members that he worked hard to promote *shalom bayit*, or peace within homes, whenever conflicts arose. In this community, which was about ninety percent *baalei teshuva,* skirmishes minor and major arose frequently with less-observant family members about participating in life cycle events. Well, if Rabbi Lapin really had some good *shalom bayit* tricks up his sleeve, now was the time to pull them out. There would be no placating Mom if he didn't come up with something!

A few days later Rabbi Lapin called with an idea: he would personally perform the actual wedding service, which included reading the *sheva brachot* (seven blessings) of the marriage ceremony and reading the *ketubah.* When he finished, he would introduce Rabbi Wise before exiting the chuppah stage right. Then Rabbi Wise would "preside" under the chuppah by speaking to the assembled. I hoped Mom would go for this because Jeff and I would technically be married by the time Rabbi Wise had his say. Would Mom realize this? I hoped not. Nervously, I offered this idea to Mom as a way to "share" the wedding honors, and thankfully Mom was happy with the arrangement. *Thank you, God!* I thought, looking heavenward, though I understood that HaShem was present everywhere, not just hovering in a celestial throne millions of miles above the Earth. Jeff and I breathed a huge sigh of relief. I admired Rabbi Lapin for devising an elegant solution to a conflict that could have grown monumentally contentious.

Jeff and I were happy and busy, planning the wedding and overseeing some minor remodeling in our condo. Our friendships at PJC were growing, and my confidence in my decision grew. I'd still be myself after we married and would grow in my Torah observance at my own pace. Together, Jeff and I would become links in the chain to Jewish tradition through the generations, a link in the chain to eternity.

Still, I had flickers of doubt. One afternoon at work, I impulsively called my friend Miriam, a female rabbi of the Reform movement, for a confidence booster. Miriam and I had been best friends for several years starting when we were teens.

Our religious worldviews were already diverging, yet I trusted Miriam completely to tell me the truth and advise me in a way that was good for me. She knew me very, very well. I looked at the sparkling diamond on my engagement ring as I picked up the phone to dial. I was grateful that she picked up the phone and immediately unburdened myself to her, sharing my insecurities about how our friends would see me, and how I would even see myself, once I "became Orthodox."

"Judy, if this is the decision you have made, you go forward and hold your head up high!" Miriam's voice was filled with conviction, and I cried with relief.

Around that time, Jeff and I went to see a traveling museum exhibition about Jewish life through the ages. It had beautiful, intricate silver kiddush cups from the 17th century, tables set as if for Shabbos with tall, filigreed candlesticks, silver *yad* ("hand") pointers used to mark the place in the unfurled parchment scroll during public Torah readings, sacred books with rare artwork inside, the small square leather boxes known as *tefillin* (which contain slips inscribed with the Shema prayer, worn on the left arm and on the head by Jewish men during morning prayers), and other artifacts. Walking through the exhibit among throngs of other visitors, I became upset.

"I don't like to see Jewish life behind glass," I said to Jeff. "Judaism is meant to be lived, not just visited in a museum. Look around. Almost no one here looks like they're observant. That means almost none of them are lighting Shabbos candles, wearing tefillin, or making kiddush Friday night. It makes me sad. I wonder how many people might take an interest in learning more just by being here?"

"I know what you mean," Jeff said. "But we'll be doing our part to keep it alive and, hopefully, take it to the next generation."

"When I was about eleven, I complained to Nana about some rule or other that Judaism made us do. And she said, 'Sveetheart, Judaism is not a religion. It's a vay of life.' I didn't get it but I never forgot her words. I think I'm only now beginning to understand it."

"That's what I'm beginning to enjoy so much," Jeff said. "It's not just a Saturday thing where we go to shul, it's part of who we are and who we become. I don't like always having to get up so early to be at the morning minyan, but I like being in shul with the other guys. And I'm still getting used to the idea of giving ten percent of my income to *tzedakah* (charity) because I didn't grow up with that idea at all, especially since my dad grew up so poor. I grew up with the idea that if I give some of my money away, I'll have less. But like Rabbi Lapin says, giving *tzedakah* creates a healthy flow of wealth in the universe. It's a 'commission' to God's favorite causes."

"That's one lesson I have liked a lot," I said. "*Tzedakah* means 'justice,' and that ten percent didn't belong to us in the first place; it belongs to the poor and needy."

As a woman, I was not obligated to join in the minyan. In fact, at any Orthodox shul my attendance wouldn't even count toward the prayer quorum. But that isn't because women are considered any less worthy than men. It's because women are excused from "time-bound" mitzvot, the assumption being that for much of their lives women have family obligations where their time is not their own. I originally resented the idea that my attendance didn't count in a minyan, but many things that didn't make sense to me at first required more investigation until I could discover the real reason for what bothered me. I was learning to suspend my own interpretations of Torah laws until I knew more than I knew now, which was, depressingly, very little.

Anyway, I sure wasn't complaining about being excused from getting up at six o'clock in the morning to attend a minyan. I had my work cut out for me already just learning to pray minimally at home alone. The complete Orthodox prayer book, including the liturgy for all three daily services plus the Shabbos and holiday services, has more than four hundred pages! I didn't see how anyone got through all the daily prayers with sustained attention.

As the wedding day drew close, Mom and I were reviewing flower options and other wedding details when she suddenly asked, "Are you really going to go to the mikveh, like my grandmother used to do in Russia?" Her tone was aghast, as if I had just confessed to kleptomania or a foot fetish.

Whoa, back to the defense bar role again, and with no warning!

I was very tempted to be snarky and say, "Yes, and I also plan to milk my own cows and *shecht* (slaughter) my own chickens, too." However, I hadn't been that brazen with my parents since I was seventeen. And they were paying for the bulk of this big, fat Orthodox wedding and had been extremely gracious about accepting it all. And "all" included inviting a boatload of people from the shul they had never even met. I needed to respond with all due restraint.

"Mom, even some Conservative married women use the mikveh," I said, pointing out that there was a ritual bath at the University of Judaism, a local Conservative institution. "Jeff and I have discussed this many times. I know this is not how you thought I'd 'turn out' and I have rethought many of my ideas. But I am now convinced that living this way will strengthen our love and our marriage. The guidelines about mikveh are part of that integrated whole." I had finally read up on the philosophy behind a woman's use of mikveh. I no longer felt it was anti-woman. In fact, I now viewed it as a way to honor the significance of a woman's reproductive life, normally something taken completely for granted.

"Suit yourselves. I just want you to be happy," she shrugged.

"I know we will."

Chapter 13

THE TALKING DONKEY

JULY 11, 1987

I MOVED INTO OUR CONDO THE WEEK BEFORE the wedding. Festively wrapped gifts were arriving steadily, and the fresh white paint on our chalet ceiling had been a brilliant idea from our friends, making our cozy unit feel much grander than its humble seven-hundred square feet. The very same week I began a new job as an editor in the corporate communications department of a Fortune 500 health care firm, which presented me with business cards printed with my name and title, as well as a company credit card to charge business lunches. Life was good.

But the day before our wedding, on Shabbos, I woke up jittery. That afternoon the women of PJC were hosting a traditional afternoon gathering for me, called a Shabbos Kallah ("Sabbath bride"). It was a low-key social event where women would share their marriage advice with me, as well as sing songs and enjoy refreshments. My mom, my sister Sharon, and a few close friends were coming, and I was eager for them to meet my new friends and show off this educated, savvy crowd, so far removed from the "Stepford Wives" of my unfair conjurings. I was honored that none other than Dr. Diane Medved would give the expected *dvar Torah*, a brief discourse either about the weekly Torah reading or a topic relevant to marriage. Diane was an accomplished author and clinical psychologist who was warm, sophisticated, and on the more "modern" side–she didn't cover her hair. I was thrilled that my non-Orthodox family and friends would see someone with her credentials in the spotlight. Perhaps they would then see that I hadn't lost my mind.

I was too nervous to eat any of the light snacks or cookies displayed elegantly on the dining room table. I was just gripping a cup of water and trying to calm down. Another writer from the shul named Liz sidled over to me. "I know what you're thinking. You're thinking, 'This is either the smartest thing I've ever done in my life or the dumbest thing I've ever done in my life.'"

I looked at her, stunned. Was I that transparent? "Don't worry," she said, smiling, "it's the smartest thing." I was grateful for her intuition, and we began to talk shop. Liz had written two books already and been published in several major magazines. I liked her and respected her professional success.

When Diane was introduced I sat proudly and more secure next to my mother and sister, sure that if anyone could put a modern, urbane, and erudite stamp on Orthodoxy, she could. I had not been in shul that morning because Jeff had his *auf ruf* (literally, "calling up"), where he was honored with reciting the blessing over the reading of the Torah. After the groom finishes the concluding blessing after the Torah is read, people will sing a quick round of "Siman Tov u'Mazal Tov," clapping hands and lobbing soft candies at him. This is a thrilling moment for the children, who dive down and begin scooping up all the candies for themselves and their friends. Custom forbade us from seeing each other this close to the wedding, so I had not been to shul that day, nor had I read the week's Torah chapter. If I had, I might not have been so utterly stupefied when Diane began to talk about the life lessons from the day's reading, which focused on the non-Jewish prophet Balaam and his talking donkey.

The smile froze on my face as Diane continued to speak, though I had zoned out, too busy thinking, *I knew about the snake. I heard about the whale that swallowed that guy Jonah. I didn't know there was also a talking donkey in the Torah. How many other talking animals are there? Why did the donkey have to open its mouth this week? Now my family and friends will no longer doubt whether I was crazy to become Orthodox. Now they'll be one hundred percent sure. Maybe they'd be right!*

I stared straight ahead, unseeing, unable to cock my head to the side to see the expressions I could just imagine on the faces of my mom, sister, and other friends. I comforted myself that while I was now certain to lose my remaining secular friends, at least I had these new friends in the community with whom I could one day try to figure out how a donkey could talk back to a prophet. My nerves, far from being calmed, were ratcheted up. After the wedding, I might need to make an appointment to talk to Dr. Medved. Not to understand about Balaam and the talking donkey, but for therapy.

The next morning, our wedding day, I nearly passed out. This struck me as very ill-timed. I mean, I had things to do.

I must confess, though, the near-fainting spell was entirely self-inflicted. My order of business of the day was first to pray and then to take a bath in preparation for going to the mikveh for the first time. My friend Sharon was also my *kallah* teacher, instructing me in many of the fundamental concepts about intimacy from a Jewish philosophical and practical viewpoint. This included the logistics of bathing and ensuring one's body was scrupulously clean before entering the mikveh. To ensure I met the standard, I planned a *hot*, relaxing bath. I could almost hear myself sighing, "Ahhhh . . ."

Rabbi Lapin had explained to us that our wedding day was

like a mini Yom Kippur, a day of fasting and bonding with God. Jeff and I would individually recite some of the same prayers as on the actual Yom Kippur, including the *Viduy* confessional. After that, God would present us with a clean slate, free of transgressions, beginning our new lives together in a state of purity. Though I wasn't thrilled about the fasting (I rarely made it even through Yom Kippur without breaking down to eat, instantly weighed down by guilt over my feebleness), I was determined to do everything right on my wedding day, including the fast, which we would break immediately after the wedding ceremony.

Since childhood, I had read the *Viduy* on Yom Kippur, but it is long, seemed repetitive, and was translated into archaic English that was difficult to relate to. Still, that morning, tummy rumbling, I did my best to focus on the prayers with a newfound intensity. I was deeply moved by the idea of our wedding day representing a new life for me, not just physically but spiritually. Standing in the living room of my new home, I read the prayers with painstaking care, wishing I understood their deeper meaning. My Hebrew was slow and halting as I sincerely asked God for His blessings to liberate me from some of my deepest regrets about some past behavior that still haunted me. I had never been wild by any stretch of the imagination, but growing up in the zeitgeist that counseled, "If it feels good, do it," I made my share of mistakes. I violated the moral standards that my parents had taught me but that could not compete on the modern campus culture, where new experiences were prized over old values.

I cried as I prayed that my marriage to Jeff would be blessed with peace, with love, with enough money to live comfortably and respectably, and with healthy children who would love Jewish values and would be spared the kind of remorse I carried with me and had dumped on several therapists' couches over the years.

After I finished the *Viduy*, my unaccustomed hunger growled into ravenousness. I tried to ignore it as I ran the hot water in the tub. I let the hottest water pour forth from the spout, watching the steam rise in the tiny bathroom. The heat from the steam made me feel lightheaded.

It was only nine-thirty in the morning, and it would be after 6 p.m. before I could eat. How would I last till then? I tried to dip my toe into the tub but had to yank the reddened appendage out of the scalding water. I added cold water and tried again, but frankly, I could have boiled eggs in that tub. I repeated the recipe of dumping out hot water and adding more from the cold tap, impatient to get on with my wedding day duties. I forced myself painfully down into the cauldron.

Big mistake. Instantly I felt weak, woozy, and witless. What was I thinking? I was supposed to bathe for cleanliness, not to *kasher* myself in boiling water. I realized I had to get out of that tub while I could still rise on my own before fainting like a fool and needing to go to a burn center. I managed to slip into a robe and leaned on the side of our kitchen table while I called our downstairs neighbor, Sarah, another shul member. "I think I'm going to faint," I whispered, and within ten seconds I heard Sarah bolting upstairs. I unlocked the door for her and fell onto the couch.

Sarah took one look at me and gave me some water, then called Rabbi Lapin to report my condition. He told Sarah that my fast was over and to give me something to eat. Sarah stayed with me while I began to recover physically, but my embarrassment at having nearly stewed myself alive on my wedding day was acute.

One of my worries in joining an Orthodox community was being watched and judged by others whose religious observance was stricter than mine. But so far, our experience had shown that the vast majority of people in the community were not judgmental, at least as far as we could discern. Jews are forbidden from nosing around or making judgments about one another short of incontrovertible evidence–a very high bar. In fact, when the Jews camped in the desert after leaving Egypt during their long wanderings, they were instructed to arrange their tents for maximum privacy, with openings out of direct view from anyone else's tent.

So while I had kicked up a fuss to Jeff about not letting the PJC community feel too close around us, that day I was immensely grateful that we lived in a building with other shul members as neighbors. Sarah's wedding morning rescue was an important lesson for me as I began my new life. Whatever the future would hold for Jeff and me, in good times and in rough times, help would be downstairs or next door or at most a block away as long as we lived in a close-knit Jewish community. And Jeff and I would absolutely want to be there to help others just as readily.

Chapter 14

DINNER WITH CHARLIE

LATE FALL 1987

THE MINUTE JEFF AND I GET HOME FROM WORK on Friday afternoon we hustle to finish preparing for Shabbos. I cook our food Thursday night, but there's still plenty to do before our day of rest begins. I set the dining table with a pretty tablecloth, our good Wedgwood china, shiny new flatware, wine goblets, Jeff's silver kiddush cup, and the large plate and cutting board for our fresh, soft challah loaves. We place the food in the oven to stay warm until dinner, leaving the oven set at a low temperature. We set the lights throughout our condo as we want them to remain until Shabbos is over. I nestle two white candles in my candlesticks, do a final quick straightening up of the apartment, and then shower and change into Shabbos clothes. Jeff will wear a suit and tie, and I will greet Shabbos in a semi-dressy skirt and blouse. At the synagogue, we welcome this day in song as Shabbos HaMalkah, the Sabbath Queen. When you are expecting royalty to arrive, you do want to look your best.

If either of us is delayed by the boss at the office, or if traffic is especially heavy, the stress can build as the minutes slip away.

Shabbos waits for no man or woman and will arrive, ready or not, eighteen minutes before the sun vanishes from the horizon. In the winter months, it's awkward to leave work at three o'clock (which, due to the necessary Shabbos preparations, will still cut it close when candle lighting is around four-thirty). A Jewish coworker galloping out of the office that early can earn dubious looks from colleagues who may be thinking, "Saturday doesn't start on Friday. What gives?" But God said, "It was evening and it was morning, the first day," which indicates that each day begins on the evening prior.

I stand for a moment and focus on my candles before I light them, still working to shift from the workweek mindset, with its concerns over article and production deadlines, to the *Shabbos* mindset and the nature of sacred time. I strike the match and light the first candle, and then the second, then wave my hands in an upward circle three times and cover my eyes before quietly reciting the blessing over this mitzvah. I wave my hands just like Mom does, and Nana used to, and as I assume all my female ancestors did throughout millennia. I don't know how this tradition started, but I feel like I'm waving in the tranquility of Shabbos. I stay rooted in my spot for several more seconds after I've made the blessing, thanking God in my own silent words for all my blessings. I exhale deeply and think: *I'm done for the week. Now is my time to rest, appreciate my life, connect to my husband, my community, and my Creator.*

Shabbat Shalom, we will greet one another throughout the day. A peaceful Shabbos.

When Shabbos arrives, we enter an island in time. Rabbi Lapin has explained that each Shabbos and holiday has its own intrinsic spiritual power, a unique cosmic character that is exclusive to that day. During this "day of rest," we will not turn the lights on or off, or adjust the oven temperature, or turn on the radio, or kill the fly that buzzed in when we opened the front door and is now circling our lunch (so aggravating!), or run to the store, or water the plants, or pick up a pen to write a note. Shabbos means *cease*. It's a day when we are meant to focus on *being*, not *doing*. I'm still learning to incorporate this philosophy, and with each passing week, I'm better able to access the calm the day brings.

Still new to this level of observance, I sometimes struggle with some of the rules. For example, a few weeks ago we realized only after Shabbos had arrived that we had forgotten to turn off a bedside lamp. I did not accept the situation with good cheer.

"Some day of rest this will be when we won't be able to fall asleep because the light is on," I groused.

"Everything we have is the way it's meant to be right now," Jeff said, covering the lamp loosely with a towel, ensuring there was enough space between the towel and the hottest part of the lamp to prevent a possible fire. The towel dimmed the room moderately, and eventually we fell asleep.

On Shabbos day we walk to the shul together. Dressed in our "Saturday best," shul members are an incongruous sight among this outré beachside population. Tourists and locals enjoying a day at the beach are dressed in shorts and bathing suits for a day on the sand. Muscle Beach is a mile down the promenade, and just east of that, the Venice Shoreline Crips are fighting a turf war with the Latino Venice 13 gang over the local cocaine trade. On the concrete strip closest to the sand, a lively flea market of sorts flourishes, with "proprietors" sitting behind folding tables selling products, services, and causes. One urges people to sign a petition to legalize marijuana. A palm reader offers to look into your future. A watercolor artist offers renderings of boardwalk scenes, including a lovely one of the front of our shul. The usual scrum of dingy homeless folks shamble around in various states of semi-cognition or sit on benches, their skin leathery from living under the relentless California sun. One showman wows the crowd by juggling chainsaws–which are on.

"So, this is where we're going to bring our future children to shul?" I ask Jeff.

"Yep, as long as we're still growing here Jewishly," he says. Most of the children in the community are still very young and apparently take this bizarre bazaar for granted. I'm not sure how healthy it will be to expose little kids to all this, but we're several years away from that reality. Looking up and down the boardwalk, it's hard to believe that as late as the 1950s, more than ten synagogues faced this stretch of the Pacific Ocean. Now, the Shul on the Beach, nearly forgotten before Michael Medved and Rabbi Lapin revitalized it, is the only one left.

I have a favorite moment each week in shul, and it was always my favorite moment, even in the Conservative shul where I grew up. It is the moment after the Torah chapter has been read aloud, its parchment scroll carefully rolled up and wrapped in its velvet mantel, its silver crown placed atop the wooden roller. The Torah is "dressed" like royalty, and in the presence of royalty, we all stand as it is carried back to the *aron,* the large wooden cabinet that houses it, by someone selected for this honor. As the Torah is placed in the *aron,* everyone sings, "*Eitz Chayim He,*" a slow melody that rises and falls. The last verses translate:

"It is a tree of life for those who grasp it, and its supporters are praiseworthy, Its ways are ways of pleasantness, and all its paths are peace."

During the final line, the melody grows more poignant, even urgent, the notes nearing the soprano range:

"Bring us back, HaShem, to you, and we will return. Renew our days as of old."

Singing together, our voices rising in pitch and intensity, I am so moved by this plea that I can hardly get the words out because I am crying. This is the moment when I feel the sweep of our storied, incomparable history, being part of the smallest of peoples who have inexplicably had the largest of impacts. I visualize my ancestors throughout the centuries carrying this same Torah, both ancient and contemporary, forever dressed in majesty. Here we still are, still keeping the faith and still looking to the Torah to show us how to live with dignity, morality, tenacity, meaning, and purpose. This moment stays with me and fuels my soul for the rest of the week.

A few months after our wedding, we hosted a very special guest for Shabbos, a man whose influence had changed the course of Jeff's life. Charlie and Jeff had met at the beginning of their junior year abroad at Lancaster University and became unlikely pals. At twenty years old Jeff was still completely secular, while Charlie was openly and devoutly Christian. With a last name that was a synonym for Christmas, majoring in religious studies, and having grown up on a street called Trinity Lane, Charlie was someone whom Jeff planned to give wide berth.

Charlie may have been God-centered in a way that made Jeff flinch, but he was also authentic, warm, intellectually curious, athletic, and endearing. Jeff found it impossible not to like him. Soon the two of them were hitting the local pubs together, enjoying rounds of ale while talking about politics, the social issues of the day, books, music, and anything else that came up. Well, *almost* anything else.

"Charlie said that we each had a purpose and that I was unique and different because I was Jewish," Jeff had told me on one of our first dates. "I rejected that. I didn't see that my Jewishness had any implications for my life, but Charlie saw me as part of the Chosen People. I cut him off and told him not to talk to me about it."

Charlie backed off. They continued to jog together around the campus in the picturesque Lake District, pounding rain showers notwithstanding, attended symphonies and plays at the university, and gave a new meaning to the term "hop-Scotching" while on a jaunt to Scotland. Charlie occasionally tested the waters and tried to talk about God, but Jeff wouldn't bite. Still, when Charlie learned that Jeff had no plans for the upcoming spring break he asked, "Why don't you go to Israel?"

Israel was nowhere on Jeff's radar screen. He didn't admit to Charlie that he wasn't sure he could even name its capital.

"You've been to Switzerland, Germany, and Spain. Why *wouldn't* you want to go to Israel? This is the land of your heritage!"

With nothing planned for the break and no good excuses, Jeff wrote to the Kibbutz Representatives of London, who arranged for him to stay on a kibbutz run by secular, even anti-religious Israelis. Jeff was surprised to discover that he was the only Jewish volunteer there. Almost everyone else was European, working in exchange for room and board while sightseeing on weekends. For two weeks Jeff worked in the chicken coop, wondering how this smelly, dirty experience connected to his Jewish identity. One Friday one of the volunteers invited him to go with him to Jerusalem for the evening. Apparently, there was something interesting to experience at a place called "The Wall."

To Jeff, *The Wall* was a Pink Floyd album. He had no idea that this wall had been the outer wall from Jerusalem's ancient Temple, destroyed two thousand years earlier. Standing among the throng of other visitors, Jeff felt a little bewildered.

"As little as I knew about the place, I was moved at the Western Wall," Jeff had told me on one of our early dates. "I could feel something there but I couldn't describe it." I had nodded with understanding. I had felt this same dramatic surge of emotion at the same site during my three summer trips to Israel.

To the trained eyes of the Jewish outreach professionals looking for unaffiliated Jews among the crowd, Jeff was easy to pick out as a ripe prospect. When one outreach rabbi moseyed over to Jeff and invited him to join a group of guys for a hot chicken dinner, he gladly accepted.

That was how Jeff had first arrived at Aish HaTorah, where he was taken aback by the unexpected sense of belonging he felt. During dinner, when many young men were singing traditional Shabbos songs and where Jeff recognized one guy as an acquaintance from the University of Illinois, he warmed up to the environment enough to agree to try some classes for a few days. The few days had stretched into three weeks before Jeff hit his own wall, spooked by the implications of all he was learning.

Back at Lancaster, Charlie saw right away that Jeff had returned somehow changed, and that he was having difficulty processing some of the new and sensational ideas he had encountered in Jerusalem. I sympathized when Jeff first shared this story with me. If you're going along and having a nice secular life, the prospect that the Torah is not just some dusty ancient text but is meant to guide a Jewish person's entire value system can be blindsiding. Charlie encouraged Jeff to continue studying and learning, which eventually led to Jeff's seeking out Rabbi Lapin in the Venice community.

Jeff and I joked that we had our own "holy Trinity." He had Charlie, and I had Kathy and Carol, all religious churchgoers who had applauded our respective spiritual soul searches while most of our Jewish family and friends had been diffident at best. Still, I was nervous before Charlie's visit, defaulting to the classic Jewish worry: "What will the goyim think?" Would even a religious Christian like Charlie find the structure of our Shabbos meal, the blessings before and after we ate and drank, tiresome? Would he find our discussion about the Torah reading of the week too parochial and ritualistic? Would he find us, in fact, *too Jewish*? We had also been invited to a *bris* (ritual circumcision) on Sunday morning, and Jeff was eager to bring Charlie along with us. I thought this would seem radically weird:

"Let's go, Charlie. Time to watch the mohel remove this eight-day-old baby's foreskin. Then we'll eat bagels and cream cheese!"

"Sounds great! Ya think maybe after we can drive along Pacific Coast Highway or walk along the Hollywood Walk of Fame?"

Jeff and Charlie embraced at the door, thrilled to see each other again. True to his reputation, Charlie was exuberant and gracious, every bit as genial as Jeff had described. He was tall and lanky and seemed genuinely excited at the opportunity to share a traditional Shabbos meal with a bona fide Orthodox Jewish couple. But no sooner had we sat down at our dining room table than Jeff and I looked at each other in alarm. We realized at the same moment that the wine we had put out on the table, while kosher, did not have the designation of being *mevushal* (literally, "boiled"), creating an acutely awkward situation. While Charlie was welcome to drink the wine with us, if he so much as touched the bottle after it was opened, the wine would be rendered unkosher, unfit for our consumption.

Most of the wines we had at home were *mevushal*. Oh why, *why*, the very first time we hosted a non-Jewish guest, and one to whom we owed a huge debt of gratitude, did we place on the table one of the only bottles in our possession that would make us look like total bigots?

Like so many other new-to-me concepts in observant Judaism, I did not fully understand the concept of *mevushal*. At that moment, I only understood one thing: social calamity was seconds away. My heart pounded wildly in my chest as I anticipated Charlie reaching for the wine, which I knew he would. There was absolutely no way for Jeff to put a good face on this. What could he say?

"*Ah, sorry Charlie, but if you put your big goyish paw on that wine, we'll have to dump the rest of it down the drain. Nothing personal.*" That seemed to lack a certain tact and diplomacy.

I was in fits of agony and wanted nothing more than to saw a hole under my chair and fall several hundred feet underground.

Charlie, as expected, reached for the wine, smiling in anticipation of pouring for his host. Jeff lunged for the bottle, managing to grasp it before a startled Charlie could start pouring. My face felt hot. I considered dying of embarrassment right on the spot to deflect attention away from this *mevushal* mishap. I sat there in utter and complete mortification as Jeff began to explain the special status of kosher wine, and the sacred role it plays in Jewish life.

"Wine has inherently spiritual qualities," my husband said. "When Jews drink wine they do so partly as a religious expression of praise to God. Non-*mevushal* wines have a higher spiritual status, and because of that, they were used in the ancient Temple in Jerusalem. A designation of *mevushal* means that the wine has been cooked at low heat for a brief period, and wines that undergo this process have a slightly lower spiritual stature than wines that are fermented through only natural processes. That's why non-*mevushal* wines are only handled by Jews."

Wow, Jeff handled that masterfully, I thought, allowing myself a small exhalation. I was impressed by how well and succinctly he conveyed a complicated spiritual concept. I smiled inwardly, proud of my man, but was still digging my nails into the side of my chair, expecting social immolation within seconds.

I glanced at Charlie almost fearfully from the corner of my eye. He appeared thoughtful, nodding slightly and taking his time to absorb what Jeff had said. I was still waiting for him to bounce off the chair, point to us, and say, "I knew you people were always clannish! Thanks for nothing. I'm going to a hotel!" Instead, to my total shock, Charlie flung his long arms out in a T-shape and exclaimed, "I think that's great! Jews *should* have their own wine! Of course, this makes perfect sense!" Charlie looked as if he was upset that he hadn't thought of this notion himself.

I was dumbstruck. It sure didn't make that much sense to me. Charlie and Jeff instantly became absorbed in a deep theological conversation and I sat there and said one of the first spontaneous prayers of thanks to God in my life.

That night, I believe I saw my first open miracle, and my belief in Divine Providence rocketed to new heights. With Jeff pouring the wine, we all drank *l'Chaim*, "to life."

Chapter 15

THE RITUAL BATH

LATE FALL 1987

SHORTLY AFTER CHARLIE'S VISIT, I AGREED to be interviewed for an article in the *Los Angeles Times* about women who used the mikveh. The reporter wanted Jewish women to explain why they followed this ancient ritual, and how it affected their marital relationships. Just months earlier I had still been arguing with Jeff over the extremity of the two-week sequester in our physical intimacy prescribed by traditional Jewish practice. Now I was boasting about it for a reading audience of millions. I guess God really does have a sense of humor!

"It's exciting to go to the mikveh," I told the reporter. "It's like a honeymoon night every month." My stomach did a little flip when I read my own words. Somehow they seemed more personal (perhaps *too* personal) than I had intended when answering his questions. The reporter was an acquaintance of my friend Liz, also a writer, who wasn't comfortable discussing her mikveh use so publicly. However, she rightly pegged me as someone who would easily blab. It hadn't been so easy for the reporter to find Orthodox women willing to talk. The zone of privacy is marked very closely in Jewish religious circles, unlike in the secular world, where people increasingly gabbed and even bragged about the most intimate things in their lives on daytime TV talk shows.

"The more valuable something is, the more we try to protect it and keep it private," Rabbi Lapin had once explained. "That includes discussions about intimate areas of a person's life, which should be reserved for the few people directly involved. Today the entire concept of intimacy has been cheapened through overexposure. You can die of exposure, you know," he added wryly.

I realized that this meant that my interview would not be hailed in the weekly shul bulletin, but I was not deterred from talking. I wanted to share my early and positive experiences with the mikveh and also felt that doing so was one way I could make amends to the Almighty for my previous sneering attitude toward the practice. I hoped that maybe a few women who saw the article and who shared my previous misconceptions about mikveh might become more receptive to what mikveh could offer a marriage–ideally, a "honeymoon every month."

As I read the article at our little kitchen table, I felt increasingly embarrassed, struck by a late-breaking understanding of that Torah concept of *tzniut,* usually translated as "modesty" but more accurately reflecting the idea of dignified discretion. Too late! I realized as the phone rang. It was Dad.

"I just read the article," Dad said, as I held my breath. "It was, shall we say, very revealing." I could hear the smile in his voice.

Ordinarily, this sort of newspaper feature would not have captured Dad's attention, given his apathy toward religion, but with a newly Orthodox and newly married daughter, read it he did, his eyes widening when my name jumped out at him in print.

I imagined Mom being upset by the article, and knew she would not call me that day. Mom was a very private person who was probably suffering agonies knowing that all her friends would see it too, perhaps wondering how Liebe's Berkeley-educated daughter had gone so religiously retro. It was bad enough that I had returned to a practice discarded by Mom's own Orthodox-raised European mother; it was quite another thing to cheerfully discourse about it in one of the nation's most widely read newspapers.

"Um, well, I guess . . ." I stammered incoherently to Dad. Our conversation was friendly, but very short and stilted, with Dad asking about Jeff's health (fine, thanks!) and my asking how he and Mom were (pretty good, thanks!). In my family, we didn't talk about sensitive matters of any sort, least of all the building blocks of marriage or intimacy. In fact, one of my earliest and most puzzling memories was when I was six and asked my mother where babies came from. She ran out of the room with reddened cheeks, not to be seen again until dinner. Two days later, she wordlessly handed me a book from the library and ran out of the room again. On each page was a different animal family: mother, father, and baby ducks; mother, father, and baby dogs; mother, father, and baby lions, and so on throughout the animal kingdom. I liked the pictures but didn't quite see how this array of animal reproduction applied to me. Two summers later, at a camp overnight in the Los Padres National Forest, I overheard a boy in a sleeping bag two rows away loudly explaining the sordid truth about where human babies come from. His tone was completely authoritative, and I have had a horror of camping out overnight ever since.

As I drove to work that day, hoping none of my colleagues had seen the article or would ask me about it, I was still glad I had been quoted in the paper. Jeff and I were happy. I felt energized not just by my new marriage but because Jeff and I were living in a way that felt intuitively right and healthy. My life still felt "normal" and not extreme.

We were far from a level of full Jewish observance: after all, there was so much to learn, and we were taking on new commitments in religious observance slowly. But we had a growing consciousness of how the mitzvot, or commandments, created a more mindful way of living in almost every sphere of life: from our new practice of giving ten percent of our income to *tzedakah;* to weighing our words more carefully to avoid speech that might be even subtly hurtful to others; to working toward an understanding of the daily and Shabbos prayers; and in trying to elevate all our interactions with other people–whether a close relative or a busboy in a restaurant–to the level of dignity and sensitivity we saw modeled through Rabbi Lapin and many of his students. Following the laws of *Taharat Hamishpacha* and going to the mikveh were ways to actualize our fresh awareness of Jewish values and live more conscientiously through them without becoming neurotic.

It was already easy to look back and laugh about my first disastrous mikveh preparation on our wedding day. Now I enjoyed the dedicated attention I paid to myself each month during the hour before going into the mikveh. It was an unaccustomed luxury to take a long, relaxing (and not too hot!) bath before my immersion. As someone who got my first professional manicure on my wedding day, I also liked the new ritual of grooming my nails with care and going over my skin with the business side of a loofah. I was not mystically inclined. Maybe I was even mystically challenged. But as I stepped down into the warm waters of the blue-tiled ritual bath, I felt a certain sacred power envelop me. This was a divinely inspired act. It carried with it divine potential.

After I had dunked down completely under the water three times, the mikveh attendant, whose manner was both gentle and discreet, pronounced my immersions "kosher." That meant it was time for me to stand in the water, cover my chest with arms crossed, and recite the blessing over the immersion. It felt odd to recite a blessing in Hebrew in only the clothes God Himself provided, and I all but whispered the words.

Like almost every woman in the Western Hemisphere with a pulse, I had many complaints about my body: my waist was too short, my hips too wide, my ankles too thick. I never gave a second's thought to being grateful for all that my body did unfailingly and consistently. I could breathe, think, see, hear, smell, taste, touch, walk, and feel. My body miraculously converted the food I ate into energy for life, and healed itself from miserable colds with only rest and nutrition.

American culture sold women on a rigid ideal of beauty unattainable and unrealistic for virtually all females. No surprise, then, that I focused on the shallowness of my visual imperfections, and that so many women obsess over our looks and our figures. It was mad. I began to wonder why, decades after feminism had taken root in our society, editors of women's magazines (most of whom were women!) insisted on digital "corrections" on the models or celebrities who graced the covers of those magazines through Photoshop and other methods of technical manipulation. These "corrected" photos of women are wildly out of touch with reality. No wonder so many women have eating disorders and so many others are popping antidepressants.

As I stood for my last moment in the mikveh, I reasoned that if God Himself welcomed my blessing of Him covered only by these "waters of Eden," my body must have a beauty and dignity I had never given it credit for. In this way, going to the mikveh affirmed for me that my body was something beautiful, which Jeff had to reassure me of constantly because I wouldn't believe it. My body had enormous power both to attract as well as to create new life, without any digital corrections.

Since our engagement, I had continued to read more articles and books about the laws of mikveh and was reassured by what I learned. A *New York Times* reporter, Lis Harris, wrote about mikveh first from a journalistic perspective and later from a more personal one after using it herself after the birth of her second child. During her research, she had discovered a lively discussion in the Talmud (whose commentaries were all written by men) that talked about how to please a woman in bed. In an essay from her book *Holy Days*, Harris quoted an anonymously penned kabbalistic work from the 13th century called the *Igeres HaKodesh* (The Holy Letter), which instructed men: "Therefore, engage her first in conversation that puts her heart and mind at ease and gladdens her. Speak words which arouse her to passion, union, love, desire, and Eros. Never may you force her, for in such union the Divine Presence cannot abide. Win her over with words of graciousness and seductiveness. Hurry not to arouse passion until her mood is ready." If you thought Dr. Ruth was a trailblazer as a sex expert, the sages of the Talmud had her beat by about two thousand years.

But mikveh isn't all love and roses. In an essay for the book *Total Immersion*, Janet Shmaryahu, an English professor at Bar Ilan University, acknowledged that the laws surrounding mikveh are complex and can seem disturbingly intrusive into the most private realm of a couple's life. This makes it a ripe target for criticism. The very expectation that mikveh night should result in a guaranteed encounter with perfect love and joy can prompt anxiety: What if it isn't? What if that headache won't go away or one of the kids barges in complaining of an earache? What if the couple's desires aren't in sync?

I was too newly married to have experienced these difficulties and inconveniences, but it was easy to imagine some of them happening over time. Despite the Torah's emphasis on privacy, this author encouraged women to write and speak out about these issues forthrightly so that women didn't think there was anything "wrong" with them if the reality didn't match the ideal. I found all this honesty reassuring.

I especially liked how she pointed out that the laws of *taharat hamishpacha* empower the woman with the timing of sexual relations. Women let their husbands know when their periods began, and women counted the seven days until they could go to the mikveh. This isn't supposed to turn mikveh into a power trip, but to provide women with a sense of their own autonomy. "The laws of Family Purity . . . take the entitlement to and the possibility of sexual dominance out of the hands of men. . . . Judaism also designs an extensive dimension of marital life to life entirely outside of any sexual conduct," she wrote. None of this means a Jewish woman cannot be victimized by a man, but it demonstrates a right to her own space and her authority to govern what happens in her own bedroom. Given my personal experience as well as other insights I had gained from so many writers, any notion of the laws of *taharat hamishpacha* as anti-woman lost its final vestiges of influence with me.

Still, observing these laws didn't always work out so great for everybody. Another young married woman from shul, "Claire," confided to me tearfully that her husband wanted her to stop going to the mikveh altogether. "Greg" had led the charge in their relationship toward an observant Jewish lifestyle. Claire was beautiful, sweet, and gregarious, and I felt keenly for her situation. She was like me in the sense that she had fallen in love with a man who had fallen in love with a Torah lifestyle. Like me, she placed a big bet that religious observance would pay handsome dividends in a thriving marriage. And Greg had made substantial sacrifices for a Torah lifestyle, giving up performing opportunities on Friday night and Saturday, a bold and risky decision for an actor.

"I actually like the sense of personal space that I have when we're not 'on,' but it just makes Greg tense," Claire told me when we took a walk one late afternoon in the quiet neighborhood near the condo building where we were neighbors. "This was supposed to make us feel closer, but mikveh is stressing us out," she said, her eyes tearing. I listened sympathetically but lacked the wisdom to know what to say. And I couldn't tell her what Jeff and I had observed and discussed privately, which is that we watched Greg leap into observance quickly–too quickly, we believed. "Flipping out," as some called it, into rapid religious observance was dangerous. It could prove nothing more than a "spiritual crush" of sorts, and short-term inspiration is easier than long-haul consistency. You needed time to kick the tires, go for a test drive, take things at a reasonable pace so as not to be overwhelmed by the truths in the Torah and the implications for living a life based on its guidelines. When I suggested to Claire that she and Greg speak to Rabbi Lapin about their problem, she said Greg didn't want to, that he was already adamant that they should drop the practice. Not wanting daily reminders of the lifestyle that hadn't worked out for them, this endearing and cheerful couple soon moved away from the community.

I was grateful that things were working out so well for Jeff and me, but living a Torah-based life came more naturally to some personalities than to others. Greg had seen the beauty and stability in the families he had met but plunged in too quickly, leading to buyer's remorse. I hoped–and even prayed, in my own way–that Greg and Claire would remain happy together and would stay connected to some Jewish practices. Jeff and I planned to invite them for a *Shabbos* meal or Sunday barbeque and try to maintain the relationship.

And I hoped that over time, the problems that began to plague Greg and Claire would not affect Jeff and me.

Chapter 16

CAN I STILL SAY THAT?

DECEMBER 1987

"JUDY, CAN YOU COME INTO MY office in ten minutes?"

My colleague "Rene" had buzzed me at my desk with this request. We had met while working a few years earlier at UCLA and were friendly but not close. I remained grateful to Rene for having tipped me off about the opening for the position I now had as the editor in the corporate communications department of a Fortune 500 health care company.

I was surprised to find a few other women from our department in Rene's office. We all stood as Rene sat at her desk, looking at us with an expression of sly seriousness.

"I need to know what Tony bought you all for Christmas," Rene asked. I was stunned. She *needed* to know what the boss had bought for us? What business was it of hers? A few days earlier, Tony had hurriedly and with an awkward manner presented me with a small rectangular white box wrapped with a ribbon, setting it on my desk. I opened the box to find a peach-colored silk scarf inside, immediately thinking: re-gift alert! I never wore scarves. Peach wasn't my color. Almost annoyed at having received something so useless, I stuck the box in the back of a drawer at home and waited for a re-gifting opportunity.

Rene revealed in front of this little knot of coworkers that Tony had bought her an angora sweater for Christmas, which she said had come as quite a surprise. Given the obvious expense of the present, Rene wondered what sort of gifts the rest of us had rated. I deeply resented Rene's inquiry. Five minutes earlier I hadn't cared one bit about Tony's trinket. Now I felt slighted.

Turns out everyone but Rene had received modest gifts, all trifles compared to Rene's pricey angora sweater. This incident added to my growing appreciation for the Jewish concern over gossip, or *lashon hara* (literally, "bad talk"). In the year or so since I had been studying with Rabbi Lapin and hanging out with other members of the PJC community, I had discovered that the Torah has strict guidelines about what constitutes proper speech and what easily slides into the category of damaging speech.

I was amazed and intimidated by how broadly *lashon hara* could be defined. It went way beyond obvious situations, such as dishing about someone else's divorce, money troubles, weight gain, or other difficulties. It also required paying attention to subtleties. For example, if I complimented "Monica" on a beautiful new piece of jewelry she was wearing and did so in front of "Jeannie," whom I was pretty certain was not in a position to afford that kind of jewelry herself, this was insensitive enough to fall into the category of *ona'as devarim* ("afflicting words," a close cousin of *lashon hara*). Talk about a high bar for guarded speech!

There were exceptions to the anti-gossip rule, but only when there was a justified reason for disclosure. That would include sharing intel about someone's slippery ethical values if the other person is considering going into business with him. It's also permissible to share relevant information about a potential spouse.

The safest thing to do was obviously to walk around with your mouth taped shut. It was so easy to blurt out something unintentionally hurtful or insensitive! And gossip is a national pastime, the foundation of half the magazine industry, not to mention TV and radio programs. Barring the taped mouth idea, I was trying to do a better job of not gossiping and taking more time to think about what came out of my mouth before I said it and could not take it back.

Rene's on-demand survey of our Christmas gifts was tacky, but it was not a victimless crime. I'm sure she meant no harm, yet she pointedly drew attention to her favored status with the boss–a married man. *Was Tony in love with Rene? Was something brewing between them?* Inquiring minds want to know! I left Rene's office irritated at myself even more than with her. I should have had the backbone to tell her that her question was inappropriate. The whole gift business should have been left private.

"God gave us two ears and one mouth, so we will listen twice as much as we talk," Rabbi Noah Weinberg had taught Jeff in Jerusalem, a nugget of Jewish wisdom we liked to repeat now and then to remind ourselves of the message. I saw that even in our new circles, levels of sensitivity about speech varied widely. At one afternoon party, Jeff and I were talking to a prosperous man from shul. He mentioned casually that he had recently sold one of his cars to a couple in the community, a couple that everyone realized was struggling financially. But as he related the story, he made quote marks in the air with his fingers when he used the word "sold," smiling craftily. I cringed. With that gesture and that smile, he was bragging about his exalted sense of generosity, underscoring the contrast in his position with that of this other couple, good and honest people working hard to make ends meet. His hand gesture alone was an example of *lashon hara*, I said to Jeff as we walked home.

Gossip like this is as kosher as shrimp. But in our culture, it's impossible to avoid hearing, reading, or even participating in a bit of wicked wiggle-waggle in our daily lives. Meyer, one of our friends from shul, loves to joke, "I never repeat *lashon hara.* I make sure to get it right the first time."

After the incident with Rene, I wanted to find workarounds in future situations where people were talking about other people and I didn't want to participate. But how to do so without seeming anti-social or holier-than-thou? I couldn't exactly walk around the office holding a sign warning, "Repent Ye Sinners!"

I wasn't always as deft at deflecting these situations as I hoped. When my pregnancy began to show, a department secretary sidled over to me in the break room as I was debating between a hazelnut and a mocha coffee. Swooping in close with her face uncomfortably next to mine she asked, "So, was this planned?"

"Yes, I planned to come in here and get coffee," I said, slamming the coffee pot down a little too hard. Honestly, where did Human Resources find these people?

"That's not what I meant," she said, missing her cue. "I meant, was this . . . "

"I know what you meant," I cut her off. "Uh-oh, look at the time!" I glanced at my watch. "I've got a conference call in five minutes." I had no intention of answering her busybody question. It would not have violated the laws of proper speech to have said, "That's a personal question," but I didn't trust myself at that moment not to bite back with something sharp and sarcastic. So I skedaddled, spilling a few drops of coffee on the carpet but holding my verbal fire.

The *lashon hara* challenge was already making me think twice before raising certain topics with people, even though at times I've been sorely tempted:

Does she realize that outfit is twenty years out of date?

Nice car he's driving. Wonder how much money he makes?

This is the second time Grace has shown up without her husband. Wonder what that means?

I've tried to catch myself in the act of thinking catty thoughts and practice the art of becoming gossip-intolerant. This respect for language was a huge draw for me during my first classes with Rabbi Lapin. The pen may not always be mightier than the sword, but words matter. Words have a life force of their own, and we need to respect their power.

Chapter 17

HI, MY NAME IS JUDY AND I'M A RELIGIOUS FANATIC

FALL 1989

NOW THAT I HAVE ORTHODOX BONA fides, including two sets of dishes (one for dairy; the other meat), forswearing shopping on Saturdays, and owning (and even beginning to read) an unabridged Hebrew prayer book, have I become a religious fanatic?

To listen to a couple of other Members of the Tribe I encountered twice in one week, the answer is a resounding yes. As Exhibit Aleph (or A), I offer the following illustration: I was in line at a bakery on Friday, waiting to purchase some challahs for Shabbos. As usual for a Friday morning, the bakery was crowded, and I was growing impatient as customers debated leisurely over the familiar varieties of challahs, Danishes, cakes, and cookies. The gentleman ahead of me could not decide among a dozen types of round frosted cakes.

"Are you sure all these cakes are kosher?" he asked the clerk. "I'm taking this to my sister's house, and if it's not one hundred percent kosher she'll throw me out! They're fanatic!" The clerk assured her nervous customer that everything in the bakery was kosher. As evidence, she sealed the cake box with a large sticker printed with the bakery name and its kosher symbol or *hechsher*. The customer visibly relaxed.

A few days later it was déjà vu all over again. I was waiting at the takeout counter of Pico Kosher Deli, where the meats are sublime and the aroma of fragrant brisket could induce hunger even in a diehard vegan. In an almost exact replay of what had happened at the bakery, the customer ahead of me asked for proof that the meat was from a trusted kosher establishment.

"This is for my son and daughter-in-law," she explained to the clerk, "and there can't be any question about where it came from. They're fanatics!" The meats were swaddled snugly in clear cello paper and then white butcher wrap, sealed with the deli's sticker, showing its name and *hechsher*. The customer tucked a couple of the deli's business cards into the brown paper bag for good measure.

I smiled as I heard these exchanges and was reminded of the old joke:

What's the definition of a religious fanatic?
Anyone who is more religious than I am.

According to that definition, I *was* becoming a fanatic, even to myself. Slowly, I had moved even beyond the traditions of Nana and Papa Cohen, including in the area of kashrut. The Cohens had raised my mom and Aunt Eleanor in a strictly kosher home, but over the years they relaxed their standards and began to eat fish and dairy foods in non-kosher restaurants. It was one of the accommodations they made to living what they felt was a principled yet modern Jewish life. In my home, Mom cooked with only kosher meat, but we ate meat at non-kosher restaurants, regularly and enthusiastically. No Rosenfeld ever met a medium-rare grilled steak that he or she didn't love.

Growing up, I was very aware that Jewish traditions were being shucked off like a scratchy old hand-me-down sweater you were ready to pitch into the Goodwill bag. My parents and most of their friends were first- or second-generation American Jews, a little embarrassed by their "greenhorn" parents with their Yiddish accents and Old World religious practices. I was proud that Mom held on to the kosher-only standard at home. I liked the link to tradition, and enjoyed going with her to the kosher butcher, watching her instruct the stocky man behind the big glass counter exactly which chickens and cuts of steak and roast she wanted.

"No, not that one, Sam, *that* one," she would point, in full *balabusta*-in-charge mode. I was fascinated and slightly disturbed by the sight and smell of so much raw meat, but quickly forgot my discomfort when Mom served a juicy chuck roast with soft baked onions on top, or chicken fragrant with garlic and sage, to her carnivorous crew. Sometimes the butcher made house calls, delivering large orders to our home. I was always startled when the gray-haired, burly, middle-aged man with the heavy European accent barreled through the front door, not even knocking before he entered.

"It's the BOOTCHER," he'd announce, hoisting a huge cardboard box and striding toward the kitchen to unload the goods. I averted my eyes from the red stains on his white apron.

So what made me a "fanatic" according to my brother and sister Jews? All I was doing was making sure that any cooked or processed foods I was buying had a certification of kashrut. But the kosher laws don't make sense in an obvious way the way many Torah laws do. This makes them harder to respect.

Most ethical laws are mandated by the Torah. These laws, known as *mishpatim,* govern human relationships and include: do not steal, do not spread gossip, return lost objects, have two reliable witnesses in a court case, give ten percent of your income to charity, visit the sick. These principles are intuitive and make society a kinder, more just place.

But this business of not mixing milk and meat? Of inspecting lettuce to ensure you will not eat even the tiniest insect hiding inside? The laws of keeping kosher are among the laws called *chukim*, whose rationale is not immediately obvious. Another well-known law in this category is the prohibition of blending wool and linen together in any garment. These laws preserve boundaries between things in the physical world that God has declared should not be mixed, though the deeper understanding of their purpose is not accessible to us.

Fortunately, I had already respected the values of keeping kosher long before I took on this new level of observance. Not combining dairy and meat reminds me that some things are life-affirming (represented by dairy) while others represent death (meat). I could also see that if we really are what we eat, not eating any predatory animal, bird or sea creature could have subtle spiritual implications for our psyches. Keeping kosher isn't the same as eating healthfully. A mile-high pastrami sandwich with fries washed down with a sugary soda followed by a hunk of brownie for dessert is a nutritional nightmare, but could also be one hundred percent kosher. However, it's also a mitzvah to protect and take care of the body, so eating that way might meet the letter but not the spirit of the law.

I've already been asked by curious non-Jewish coworkers about my kosher eats:

"Does that mean a rabbi blessed your food?"

Answer: Rabbinic blessings don't make anything kosher.

"Is pork still not kosher?"

Answer: Pork is still not kosher, never will be.

"I understand why the kosher laws used to be important, but with modern health laws we don't need them anymore."

Answer: The benefits of eating kosher are primarily spiritual, not physical.

While we were dating and newly married, Jeff and I ate fish or dairy in non-kosher restaurants, but our new home was strictly kosher according to the standards of Rabbi Lapin's community. At least I thought so. One morning, Rabbi Lapin called me. Sometimes he would call on a Thursday or Friday just to wish us *Shabbat Shalom*, but this was a Monday–way too early in the week for that greeting.

After his typically gracious inquiry about how Jeff and I were doing, he got down to business, which was good because a Monday call made me nervous. Something was up.

"I understand you and Jeff had guests for Shabbos," he said.

"Yes, we did," I said, now wondering, *What did I do wrong?*

"And I understand that you served chicken, along with the liver," he added.

"Yes . . ." What could be wrong with that? The liver had come in a little plastic bag inside the cavity of the chicken, which was as kosher as it could be. Nana had made fried and chopped liver all the time–something I detested but that my sister Sharon loved. I didn't understand where he was going with this. But he then explained that because uncooked liver still has blood in it, it needs to be broiled first to ensure that no speck of blood remains when it is cooked. Nana never explained that to me. I'm sure she just did it.

I was mortified. Despite my best efforts, I had actually served a meal that was in some ways *treyf* because of the blood from the liver. How did anti-Semites ever effectively manage to spread the blood libel against Jews, when ingesting blood is one of the most *treyf* things imaginable? Well, logic and reason have never been strong suits of the rabidly anti-Jewish.

"So how about if you come over and Susan can review some basics about kosher cooking?" he said.

"I'm so embarrassed. I didn't know." Would those guests ever come to us again?

"I fault myself," he said. "I should have made sure Susan had spent some time with you to help with all this." Well, hey, if the rabbi wanted to take some of the heat off me, I was fine with that. Two nights later, Susan cheerfully provided a Kosher 101 class in her kitchen, as I took notes. I was pleased that most things she showed me I already knew from my months of staying with Sharon and David, and from observing what went on in the kitchens of other homes where we had been guests. Fortunately, our reputation survived, unsullied, and once I got up the nerve to invite people over again, our invitations were accepted.

Eventually, about a year after we were married, Jeff wanted more consistency: he wanted to keep kosher not just inside our home but outside as well. I was not ready for this and grumbled inwardly that he was always a step or two or even three ahead of me in spiritual growth. There went our leisurely Sunday brunches at our favorite bistro, or meeting our parents for dinner at The Cheesecake Factory. I wasn't the only one who was miffed.

"This is extreme," my father-in-law argued when Jeff told him that in the future we'd be able to dine out with them only in kosher restaurants.

"I'm sorry you feel that way, but this is the standard we are keeping now," Jeff said. "We're lucky here in L.A.–there are several nice kosher restaurants. We won't lack for places to go."

"That isn't the point," Bob said. "You're narrowing your options and getting too insular. Like I said, you're getting extreme."

Jeff didn't back down, and fortunately Bob was able to discover the joys of the kosher deli and a few fine restaurants. I did respect Jeff's desire for consistency but was in no hurry to match him in this area. I wasn't ready to sever this link with my secular life, and happily continued occasionally to dine out for lunch with friends.

Unexpectedly, that all changed. One day, after a business meeting that went long, I felt cross-eyed with famine. I also had a serious craving for a tuna melt and fries, my favorite comfort food lunch. Tantalizingly close to the office was a good fifties-style café, and I raced over. I sat ravenous until my food arrived, feeling that I hadn't eaten in three days. Before the waitress had fully set my plate down, I had grabbed the hot sandwich and started tucking into it, savoring the melted mozzarella slipping down the side of the crisp grilled sourdough bread. But my gastronomic rapture was short-lived. Not five minutes into my meal, I was seized by a bizarre and inexplicable pain shooting through my left arm and up into my neck.

I stopped eating, alarmed and perplexed. I was certain I wasn't having a heart attack, but where had this pain come from? I had not strained any muscle recently or had any injury. I tried to nibble at my sandwich, but the pain was intensifying. Was this some sort of message from above? Nah, couldn't be! But why was this happening right after Jeff's and my conversation about no longer eating out at non-kosher places? Didn't God have much more important things to do than attend to my midday meal habits?

I wasn't superstitious, but this pain was so strange, the timing so eerie, that I couldn't help but wonder: *Hello? I know this is probably unlikely, God, that You are by some chance sending me a message about my eating in* treyf *restaurants, but do you think you could take this pain away? I can barely turn my neck, and I'm already a member of a very stiff-necked people! Anyway, God, it's only tuna!*

The Almighty did not send any obvious reply, such as a toy-sized aircraft scribbling a message in a plume of smoke: "*Why yes, that was Me! Glad you're catching on!*" Too spooked and in too much pain to finish my meal, I paid my bill and drove back to work. The pain subsided agonizingly slowly, only fully dissipating about five hours later–about the time it would have taken for my body to have fully digested the meal.

Over the next few days, I wondered what, if anything, this episode had meant. Was I simply being irrational and gullible? Or was God in fact communicating with me in a way I would be foolish to ignore? I decided that even if this freak spasm was simply a total coincidence, I still had the choice to see a lesson in it for me. That's what I decided to do. This incident was no Last Supper, but I decided to make it a Last Luncheon for me in a non-kosher restaurant.

In Rabbi Lapin's Thursday night class he happened to mention that in Hebrew the concept of "coincidence" does not exist.

Chapter 18

HAIR TODAY, HIDDEN TOMORROW

NOVEMBER 1991

I'M TRYING ON A PARADE OF FALSE MANES in a Beverly Hills wig salon–something I had sworn I would never do. But here I am, flirting with wigs both straight and wavy, pixie short to shoulder length, medium chestnut to dark brunette.

I brought Sharon along to help me decide among the styles–and to keep me from chickening out. Sharon is a calm and steadying influence, and in case I panic during my first wig purchase, I have deputized her to act in the role of therapist. Sharon, a longtime veteran of wearing wigs (*sheitels* in Yiddish), offers helpful critiques of each topper, ensuring that I won't accidentally walk out with anything on my head that looks like it was styled by a taxidermist. These wigs are synthetic, lighter both literally and financially than real human hair wigs. This makes them very appealing. On the other hand, many synthetics look suspiciously bloated and stiff, refusing ever to obey the laws of gravity. They practically scream, "YES, THIS IS A WIG!"

I may have spurned the idea of *sheitel*-wearing for myself over the last few years, but all the while I was clandestinely studying the wigs other women were wearing for verisimilitude. If you ever want to put a huge smile on the face of a married religious Jewish woman, just go up to her and say, "I cannot believe that's a *sheitel.* It looks so *real*!"

"This one looks really nice," Sharon enthuses, as I turn my head from left to right and back again, assessing the realism quotient of the shoulder-length, wavy dark-brunette number. It's much longer and, of course, fuller than my own short layered cut, a style I have not varied since I was a teenager.

"It's pretty, but I feel like an impostor," I say. "I could go on a mission to Serbia for the CIA in this thing. All I need are dark shades and a smart trench coat to go along with it."

Sharon laughs. "Sometimes it's nice to feel a little different than your natural look. But, hey, no pressure from me!"

I don't love any of the wigs but will pick something today, probably this one, so I can finally wear hair to weddings and other dressy occasions, rather than a hat or beret. I have already spent a tidy packet on the hats, scarves, and berets (some from an upscale designer) purchased since making the momentous decision several months ago to finally take my locks undercover. I rationalized my expenditures as the price for taking on a mitzvah that I found so challenging. God would understand my womanly need to feel pretty while I kept my hair under wraps *for the rest of my life*. Right?

After all my bellyaching about it, I was surprised that it wasn't nearly as hard a transition as I expected. Throwing on a beret before heading out the door each day makes me feel slightly bohemian and pleasingly ethnic, and the hats add panache to my otherwise minimalist style. Under a hat or beret, I still feel and look like me. But a wig, I knew, would transform me unmistakably into an Orthodox woman, someone who is *frum*, a Yiddish word that means "pious" but has become synonymous with straight-arrow, rightwing Orthodoxy. I don't identify with this label, and that's why I delayed taking this step.

I also feared that the weight and closeness of a wig hugging my scalp would exacerbate my chronic migraines, a lifelong plague. I needed to add to my migraine triggers like I needed, well, a heavy wig on my head. And unlike hats, wigs need regular maintenance.

"It's like a pet," my friend Esther Chana joked about *sheitels*. "You need to wash it and groom it and speak nicely to it and sometimes even take it for walks for it to behave. But at least when you get dressed you don't have to match your outfit to your hair."

Despite my misgivings, I write the check for the wavy number, thinking, *You have now officially joined The Other Side*.

I feel some chagrin as I tote my new hair home. Naturally, it's always the people like me–those who protest and argue most vehemently–who usually end up giving in to whatever they had been protesting and arguing about in the first place. During my first few years living in the Venice community, my view on this sensitive topic had evolved, and I transitioned from the stance that I would never cover my hair–ever–to at least *wanting* to want to do the mitzvah.

Most of the mitzvot I had accepted on myself had been relatively easy. The toughest one so far had been no longer eating in non-kosher restaurants, something I still miss at times, especially when walking by a crowded outdoor café and watching carefree diners tucking into their beautifully presented salads and sandwiches, and hearing the gentle clinking sounds of their glassware meeting the tabletop. Covering my hair demanded much more effort and sacrifice. It was a tall order to use my free choice as a means to relinquish another free choice, but based on my experiences so far integrating more Torah practice in my daily life, I believed it could help me grow closer to God as a result.

No rabbi, teacher, or acquaintance had ever even hinted that I cover my hair. And while hair covering is also a mitzvah from the Torah just like keeping kosher and observing Shabbos, this practice has not been universally observed by Orthodox married women. Rabbinic opinions about hair covering have varied widely as to how much hair should be covered and in what circumstances. Despite this lack of clear-cut rules, I still wanted to understand this mitzvah and why my friends had signed up for it. Sharon is one of the few community members who grew up Orthodox, but neither her mother nor her mother's friends covered their hair other than wearing a hat to shul.

"It wasn't an easy transition for me," Sharon told me frankly. "But it was important to David, so I went along. I learned to appreciate the mitzvah over time, but I can't claim I'm in love with it."

However, my friend and next-door neighbor Carol had a different view. "I couldn't wait to cover my hair," Carol had told me a few years earlier, when we were both new mothers and I had dropped by for one of my frequent visits with my baby, Avi. As friends and next-door neighbors, Carol and I enjoyed many hours together each week, talking while taking care of our babies, either in one of our apartments or on outings to the mall or a park. Carol's colorful scarves and the beautiful *sheitel* she wore on Shabbos perfectly framed her pretty face. While Jewish law, *halacha,* allows a small amount of hair to show (a measurement known in Aramaic as a *tephach,* equal to about the breadth of four fingers), Carol has always been stringent. I never saw even the slightest bit of fringy bangs peeking out from under her scarves.

"I love the Torah's philosophy that a woman's hair is considered her crowning beauty, and that after marriage it becomes something special and private that only her husband can see. I also like how it marks a boundary between me and the rest of the world, almost like the mezuzah on our doors marks the boundary between our private, internal space and the outside world," she said.

"Well, but what about the old 'hat hair' effect? After a full day under a wig or scarf our hair may not look so beautiful anymore," I noted practically. "Seems to me if we want to look beautiful for our husbands we might need to keep it covered till the lights are off!"

"Judy, you can brush your hair and even wash it in the evening!" Carol retorted, long accustomed to my "devil's advocate" tendencies. "For me, covering my hair reminds me that my focus is on my internal life and not to emphasize externalities. I like going out in the world and feeling that I am living the way HaShem wants me to live."

"What about those crazy expensive, super-long, sexy wigs that make a woman look like she's trying to look like a celebrity? In that case, the woman's own hair would really seem like a disappointment to her husband. Doesn't something like that defeat the purpose?"

"There I agree with you," Carol said, lifting her daughter, Sara Hanna, into the highchair for a lunch of scrambled eggs and soft-cooked carrots. Avi was still absorbed on the floor with building a tower out of colorful, plastic stackable blocks. "Those wigs might adhere to the letter of the law but it's hard to see that they keep the spirit of the law. Jewish women should dress attractively but not to the point of being provocative."

Everything Carol explained made sense, and I admired–even envied–her love of this mitzvah. I hoped one day to "make it my own," as Jeff often said about levels of religious observance, to feel a real connection with this mitzvah. On the other hand, I also didn't want to remain a stubborn holdout.

For the next few years, I continued to meditate over the issue, still on the hunt for true inspiration that would help me finally commit. But one day I saw something that unexpectedly rattled me, and convinced me that if I ever took this on, it was for keeps. No trial basis.

One morning, I saw "Abby," a shul member who lives in our

pocket of the neighborhood, leaving her house and getting into her car. Till then, Abby had dressed in a strictly kosher, buttoned-up way, with long sleeves and skirts or dresses that fell a bit below the knee. Her hair was always bundled under a scarf, a snood, or a wig. That day, Abby's hair was uncovered.

I was stunned, riveted by the sight of her hair. I tried not to stare. How did that feel, I wondered, having the ocean breeze from a mile and a half away blowing through her curly locks, after years of having it bound under a wig or scarf? Abby looked straight ahead as she got into the car and drove away, though I must have been in her peripheral vision at the beginning. Did she feel more awkward or liberated to have flipped her wig while part of the community, I wondered?

More questions flooded my mind fast and furiously: was it only hair covering that Abby couldn't take anymore, or was her religious lapse more far-reaching? Was her marriage to "Jerry" in trouble? I couldn't possibly know the extent or source of her unhappiness, but my gut told me that ditching the wig was probably a symptom of a deeper distress. After all, uncovering her hair was such a public repudiation of this mitzvah, though there was no private way to repudiate it, either. I also suddenly recalled that more than once I had seen Abby and Jerry in the Lapins' living room on Thursday night after the class, waiting for their turn to consult with him. I remember that Abby appeared careworn, even anxious, but at the end of a long day where she was taking care of her young children, I assumed she was justifiably tired.

The day I saw Abby with her hair uncovered, I realized how naïve I still was and, unfortunately, still somewhat arrogant, too. How could I assume that the people around me at shul, in classes, or at a picnic were all happy campers here in *baalei teshuva* land? I was so absorbed with my own issues of religious commitment that I didn't stop to consider how others might also be struggling with their spiritual beliefs and practice. Who knew what conflicts, perhaps disappointments, lurked beneath the surface?

The shock of seeing Abby that day also demonstrated how quickly I had become sheltered. How absurd that I took for granted the sight of the half-clothed and often half-crazed regulars on the boardwalk near our shul (sometimes they staggered inside), but was shaken by the sight of a totally normal woman, otherwise conservatively dressed, because her hair was uncovered! It was almost comical.

I was desperately curious about Abby and Jerry's situation, but following the laws of *lashon hara*, I couldn't ask anyone. The only person I could discuss it with was Jeff. Even when we discussed other people privately, we tried to uphold the standards for proper speech, first discussing whether there was a constructive reason or larger purpose for talking about them. We did not want to indulge in any recreational "dishing the dirt."

"I don't know why but this really upset me," I told him. "It somehow feels like a tear in the fabric of the community. Am I overreacting?"

"Maybe," he shrugged. "It's a bigger deal for you than for me. Clearly, Abby has some things to work out, but I wouldn't read that much into it."

"I feel very bad for her, and for Jerry," I said. "There may be some serious strife in that household. I'm not judging her, but this shows me how one person's actions can have a much wider impact. Abby's making a statement that she's feeling too confined, but if seeing her this way was troubling for me, it may also be troubling for other people, too. Maybe that's why it says in *Pirkei Avot* (Ethics of the Fathers) that all Jews are responsible one for another. If and when I begin to cover my hair, it will be for keeps. It would be my mitzvah individually, but my doing it–or not–could influence other people, so its impact goes beyond just me."

"That may be true, but just remember," Jeff said, "this isn't a competition and you should only take it on if you are ready to. It shouldn't feel like a burden."

Oddly, Abby's renunciation of her hair covering made me more determined to discover a way that I could embrace it. Unfortunately, my next attempt in this area was a bust. I eagerly attended a Sunday morning lecture on this topic given by one of the city's most renowned rabbis. I wanted so much for him to inspire me that I'd run straight from that auditorium to the nearest hat store and come home with a bagful of hats, pledged and bound to hair covering forever. More than two hundred women filled the hall, most of them hair coverers already. Did they still need inspiration, too?

The rabbi earned points for being impassioned and was emphatic about the incalculable heavenly rewards for women who kept this mitzvah. He invoked the memory of Kimchi, a woman discussed in the Talmud, who as a result of covering her hair so carefully enjoyed the merit of having seven sons, each of whom served as a High Priest when the Temple stood in Jerusalem. "The rafters of her house never saw her hair!" he shouted.

I drove home in total frustration, resenting the rabbi and his message. How was I supposed to relate to an impossible role model like this Kimchi of Talmudic lore? Why should I even try? The Torah I had learned so far had taught me never to try to be like anyone else but to find my own mission that God had for me, fulfilling my unique potential. There's a line from a popular Jewish children's song that I love that says, "I want to find my letter in the Torah, the one that's meant for only me." A letter by itself has no meaning, but letters joined coherently form words, words joined together coherently form sentences, then paragraphs, then complete stories. Each Jew is an essential letter in our history's unfolding, according to Jewish mystical tradition. Beyond motherhood, which was very significant, where else would I leave my stamp on the Jewish community and the larger society surrounding it?

I also was still confused by two seemingly contradictory statements about keeping mitzvahs: On one hand, the reward for doing a mitzvah is supposed to be the mitzvah itself; in other words, we should do them for their own sake. On the other hand (because with Jews there are always at least two arguments and usually at least six), we are also told (à la Kimchi story) that doing mitzvot *does* bring rewards. Well, which one was true? I asked Jeff about this. He was always reading more Jewish law and philosophy than I was.

"This confession stays within the walls of this house," I said, "but if I began to cover my hair, I'd want some assurance that I'd get rewarded for it. Preferably a significant reward, since it would be something I would consider a sacrifice. Is that wrong?"

"I don't think so, it's normal. It's true that if you take on a mitzvah *only* for the sake of the reward, it's considered a lower level, but it's also a legitimate stepping stone on the road to doing mitzvoth for their own sake, when you'll feel more spiritually connected to them and less concerned with any reward. The root of the word mitzvah is *tzav*, which means a hook or connecting piece. Doing mitzvot is meant to help us feel connected to God."

"Well, if Kimchi didn't say no to her rewards, I sure won't say no to mine," I said, hoping God was listening and was busily planning my big reward package for when I accepted this mitzvah.

After Avi turned three years old, the topic assumed an unexpected urgency. According to Jewish tradition, on his third birthday we placed a large colorful kippah on his head with a proud flourish, and presented him with his first pair of pint-sized tzitzit, like his friends wore. He was excited by this milestone and so were Jeff and I. These were symbols that, even as a preschooler, gave Avi daily physical reminders of who he was, and of the mitzvot he was expected to learn to uphold. Naturally, as he played, running and tumbling, his kippah flew off his head at least a dozen times a day. I'd see him bare-headed and ask, "Avi, where's your kippah?" I actually felt foolish asking him.

I wondered how long it would be before it dawned on him to ask me, "Mommy, why don't you cover your hair like most of the other mommies do?" Now this was hardly the toughest question in the world, and I could deflect it easily, saying, "That's not our custom," or some alternate explanation. This might satisfy him, perhaps for years. But it wouldn't satisfy me.

So after all the discussions with friends, teachers, and Jeff, after the lectures I'd heard and the reading I'd done, this is what finally spoke to me: *My son is only three, and I'm expecting him to remember to cover his head when I'm thirty-one and not covering mine?*

I decided that to be the role model I wanted to be for my children, I wouldn't reject this mitzvah because it was "hard." Personal growth *was* hard. If I rejected everything in life on that basis, I'd probably be a fat, uneducated, selfish slob. I actually liked the challenge of self-improvement, as long as it didn't involve too many pushups or reading too much Henry James, where a little goes a long way.

I was also banking on the Torah concept of "*Na'aseh v'nishma*," meaning, "We will do and we will hear." This is what we Jews said to God on the cusp of receiving the Torah at Mount Sinai. All the major Torah commentators seized on this odd phrasing, where the order of "we will do and we will hear" seems backward. Who agrees to the terms of a contract before reading it? But we agreed to live by the Torah even before reading the large print, let alone the fine print.

"That is precisely the point," Rabbi Lapin explained when I asked him. "Psychologists understand the premise that you need to practice the desired behavior many times before you feel the emotion that you hope will come along with it. If you are not a grateful person to begin with, you can't afford to wait until you experience the feeling of gratitude to start saying 'thank you.' Saying 'thank you' every time someone does something for you will make you a thankful person."

In the four years since I had married Jeff, I had allowed my sense of identity to evolve, changing both from the inside out and the outside in. Slowly and very incrementally, I was inching toward a greater observance of the laws of *tzniut*, subtly changing the way I dressed. Hair covering would be a natural extension of that. When translated awkwardly as "modesty," *tzniut* can sound downright prudish, even Victorian. But like so many Hebrew words, it cannot be translated simply with another single word. It is *a de-emphasis of the physical self in favor of a greater emphasis on the person inside*. Practically speaking, it involves dressing, speaking, and behaving in a distinguished, discreet manner. Ideally, women dressed in a *tzniut* way express their own, individual allure, one that emphasizes their dignity and feminine mystique. To hear people talk, you'd think it was something that only obligated women, but it applies equally to men.

Now *this* was an idea that had clicked with me immediately.

Ever since that dark day when I was six years old, spending a day at the beach with my family and suddenly roped into an impromptu bathing suit contest for little girls, stage-managed by a local radio station, I had recoiled at the idea of having my figure evaluated for public consumption. I was acutely uncomfortable standing there in the sand under the glare of the sun as the radio show host viewed and discussed us all one by one, finally declaring us all "winners." Today, no radio station would try such a thing, but overall I think the situation now is worse for girls than it was then. Girls are taught to equate their physical beauty with their value, both overtly and covertly.

You bet I was thrilled to reject this shallow, damaging mindset and sign on to my own value system instead!

But like any normal woman, I always wanted to be seen as beautiful and desirable, yet not to be ogled. Once when I was single I bought a form-fitting outfit in a hue of dazzling blue. I wore it a few times to parties, hoping to boost my lagging self-esteem. I knew the outfit had worked when one young man saw me walk into the room and stared, his beer beginning to dribble down his shirt. Okay, fine, I *did* enjoy that moment for the comedic value and the "compliment," but I also felt my cheeks redden, and I was embarrassed at the same time. I wanted to be judged as a whole person, even if it meant I didn't get as much attention from the opposite sex. Besides, how can you be judged as a whole person if you're only half-dressed? At a certain point, dignity requires fabric.

I used to consider *tzniut* as another way to repress Jewish women. Now I see it as a gift. I am liberated from any social pressure to compete with other women in dressing to stimulate men. It also allows me to make a quiet statement about my countercultural values. I also think it's a gift for men. Provocatively dressed women are everywhere, even–often–at the workplace, training men to view women as sex objects and not whole human beings. And everyone knows that men are intensely visually driven!

Jeff sometimes has challenging situations in this regard. One day he came home and told me about a woman who came into his signage and graphics company and tried to explain to him the type of lettering she wanted on a sign. Unfortunately for Jeff, her "Exhibit A" was the tight T-shirt she wore, emblazoned with her lettering of choice. She kept pointing to her front acreage and saying to my husband, "Look! I want it to look like this!"

Poor Jeff! He is one of the universe's last genuinely innocent men. He tries hard to avoid getting too close physically to any woman except me and to keep a respectful distance from women who are calling attention to their sundry physical assets. Doing his best to avoid close encounters with the customer's personal real estate, Jeff managed to write up the order and even got her desired font recorded properly!

This customer has a lot of company in terms of fashion statements. Many women today dress in a style that reminds me of most health insurance policies: there's so much that isn't covered. "Undignified" is not the look that I imagine most women are after, but when so much private real estate shows or is tightly encased in spandex, men and women become numb to the impact that exposed feminine beauty should excite. That can't be a good thing. We don't have to dress like Puritans at the first Thanksgiving, but I have a hunch that women could more easily command the respect they want if they dressed with a bit more yardage.

Since department stores and most boutiques are not exactly bursting with traditionalist clothes, shopping can resemble a treasure hunt. On a happier note, though, when I do shop with one of my friends from shul, we share the thrill of discovery when we spot that elusive garment that is pretty and chic and modest, all at the same time. We can be heard calling to one another from the next clothing rack, "Look what I found! Sleeves!"

It's exciting moments like this that can almost make you forget that your pretty *sheitel* has just started to itch.

Chapter 19

THROUGH A CHILD'S EYES

WINTER 1993

"GRANDMA, ARE YOU JEWISH?"

My stomach lurches as Avi, three-and-a-half years old, hollers to my mother after Shabbos lunch. My mom had joined us that day without Dad–who was at a UCLA football game–and has already crossed the front lawn, car keys poised in readiness to drive home, when Avi suddenly darts after her.

Jeff and I have known the day would surely come when our kids began to notice that their grandparents, aunts, uncles, and cousins didn't keep kosher or go to shul on Shabbos and asked why Papa and Grandpa didn't wear a kippah. We have prepared a few phrases in advance, including, "Nana and Papa weren't as lucky as you are to have learned so much Torah when they grew up." We were aiming for explanations that were nonjudgmental and age-appropriately simple, while still reinforcing our value system.

But kids say the darnedest things at the darnedest times, and I never imagined that the opening salvo in this sensitive topic would emerge almost as a challenge to my mother's very identity as a Jew. *Oy va voy!* Would Mom be ticked off? Would she somehow hold us responsible for implanting such subversive ideas into Avi's head?

Without missing a beat, Mom answers Avi laughingly, "If I'm not, you're not!" She waves as she gets into her car and we wave back from our front lawn. She drives off smiling.

Avi is too young to understand Mom's answer: Jewish identity is defined by matrilineal descent. Still, he asks no further questions. Yet.

"Mom really nailed that one!" I marvel as Jeff and I clear the lunch dishes from the table. Despite Mom's rapid-fire, witty, and good-natured response, I'm still calming down inside, feeling I dodged a bullet.

"She sure did," agrees Jeff, beginning to sweep under the dining room table. "Glad she didn't take it the wrong way."

"We're fortunate our parents have been as accepting as they have been, all things considered," I say. "They didn't like it when we stopped going to non-kosher restaurants with them, but they got over that. We both know of situations where our friends are much more often on the defensive about keeping Shabbos and kosher."

One of the thorniest problems that *baalei teshuva* face is how to involve our less-observant family members in our lives in a way that demonstrates our love and respect (for our parents in particular), while also steadfastly following halacha. Jeff and I are committed to modeling the mitzvah of *Kibud Av V'eim* ("honoring your father and mother") and passing that on to our kids, with no regard for differences in our religious practice. I realized before we married, though, that to keep that connection strong, my writing life would have to make way not only for motherhood–I hoped–but also a whole lot of cooking. Given our kosher requirements, I'd be the chief cook and bottle washer every Shabbos, holiday and even Fourth of July meals when our extended family joined us. Our parents come over often, and I have learned to conduct a cooking symphony in my kitchen, with slotted spoons and spatulas as my batons. My oven mitts bear the battle scars from their forays inside the giant maw of my oven set at 375 degrees.

I don't *always* cook for family get-togethers. Sometimes we bring deli or Chinese (Jews' second favorite take-out option) to one of our parents' homes for a casual Sunday dinner, but take-out on a holiday would be downright sacrilegious. Besides, how cruel would I be to deprive the family of my famous sweet and savory Rosh Hashanah brisket? No, some things are just beyond the pale.

Avi's jarring question about his grandmother's lineage wasn't the first time he had shown me how he sees the world through an entirely Jewish lens. Last December, I took a walk in our neighborhood with Avi and our second son, Noah, two years old and happily riding in the stroller. Turning down a side street, we approached a house whose owners set up a nativity scene on the front lawn each year: the full manger, with baby Jesus in a small basket, mother Mary stage left, three wise men stage right, and two camels. To me, there was no other possible interpretation of this scene than as a thoroughly Christian nativity. But Avi's immersive Jewish life, including Jewish preschool, made this a fascinating Rorschach test. He saw something else entirely.

"Look, Mommy! There's baby Moshe, Batya, and two *g'malim* (camels)!"

I suppressed a laugh but was delighted to suddenly see the scene through his eyes: Moshe (Moses) as a baby, saved from certain death in the Nile by Pharaoh's daughter, Batya. During the Jews' long enslavement in Egypt, Pharaoh had decreed death on every newborn Jewish male. In an act that was part desperation and part faith, Moshe's mother, Yocheved, had woven a waterproof basket for her newborn son and hidden him in the bulrushes of the Nile. Pharaoh's daughter rescued the baby and raised the future leader of the Jewish people right under Pharaoh's nose in the palace.

"Well, you don't often see that in the neighborhood!" I said, touched at Avi's analysis of the tableau in front of us.

Parenthood is the ultimate game changer. When I first became a mother, the world suddenly took on a sinister cast, with dangers to my child lurking in too many places. Child-proofing outlets and moving cleaning solvents out of reach was just the beginning. I would cross to the other side of the street with my child if I decided I didn't like the surly expression on the face of the guy sauntering toward us. Even before my children could understand the words, I'd fume when people liberally peppered their everyday conversations with obscenities, something that was more and more frequent.

Beyond safeguarding their physical safety, Jeff and I need to somehow stay a step ahead of them in terms of our Jewish worldview. My children will grow up with a fluency in Hebrew–even Aramaic!–that will leave me far behind. Now I'll have something else in common with my Cohen grandparents–raising children in a new culture where Torah values and the lingo of Orthodoxy will prevail. Now who's the immigrant?

By fourth grade, my kids will know more Torah "inside" the text than I do, and will already have begun learning the indispensable 11th-century Torah commentary of Rashi, written in a unique Old French script. Our sons will also begin learning Gemara, the rabbinic discussion and commentaries that comprise what is known as the Talmud (Oral Torah). If I have daughters, they are likely to learn mostly from among the twenty-four books of what is known as Tanach, an acronym for Torah, *Nevi'im* (Prophets), and *Ketuvim* (Writings). These include Proverbs, Psalms, Ecclesiastes, Esther, Song of Songs, and many other sacred texts.

Naturally, I have asked why only boys and not girls study Gemara. One explanation I have heard is that most boys are naturally better suited to grappling with the particular logic used by the rabbis in Gemara, along with the sometimes aggressive *shakla vetarya* (give and take, in Aramaic). This *shakla vetarya* is the boisterous verbal jousting that students engage in as they debate the meaning of what the rabbis of the Talmud had explained. No wonder there have always been so many Jewish lawyers: our people have been debating the finer points of law for more than three thousand years!

I am not ready to concede this point about girls being less suited to Gemara learning, but in the past few years I've also learned to suspend judgment until I have more facts and experience at hand. Little boys sure play differently than little girls, and their brains are wired differently, too. For now, I don't have to worry: my boys are very little, and I have a big cushion of time before having to decide this educational direction. If we still disagree years from now, we can send our children to a more liberal school where girls will also have the option to learn Gemara.

By that time we will have added to our home library the tall, thick tomes of Talmud that my Papa Cohen had in his home, and which Rabbi Lapin has in his study. These thirty-six tractates of the Talmud are densely packed with rabbinic debate and have been in constant circulation since the 3rd century. That's some impressive publishing track record! Most observant Jewish homes worth their kosher salt have these books, and even though neither Jeff nor I may ever be able to read through them, just having them displayed adds to the aura of a Jewishly literate home.

It's a little intimidating, knowing we'll be raising kids whose Jewish IQ will outstrip ours before their orthodontic braces are on. But Rabbi Lapin and his wife, Susan, who both grew up Torah-observant, take pains to reassure us that we're not exactly know-nothings and to beware the tendency to shortchange what we have learned in front of our kids. One night when she was teaching a class based on the Rambam (Moses ben Maimon, the 12th-century rabbi from Spain and one of the foremost Jewish thinkers of all-time), Susan advised, "Even when your kids can read and understand better than you can, and even when they know more halacha than you know, don't ever think–or let them think–that they know more Torah than you do. Torah knowledge is more than just laws or knowing verses by heart. It's also the understanding of what it means to have a Torah personality and the refinement that comes along with that. You as a parent will always have that more than they do until they're grown up."

This was very reassuring. And while I'll be no match for our kids in terms of Torah literacy, I believe I will be able to match them, if not beat them, in my enthusiasm for text-based study. For example, when I heard about an opportunity for women to get together and learn in pairs *chavruta*-style, as men usually do, I couldn't wait to go.

The event took place at a synagogue over in the Pico-Robertson neighborhood, whose Orthodox population continued to grow almost exponentially. The room had been set up with a series of long tables so that each pair of students would sit across from one another as they discussed the text they had chosen. Everyone quickly found partners, and soon the room was humming with the sounds of about forty women reading Hebrew and discussing what the commentaries had to say. I paired up with a woman named Rose, who had studied in a seminary in Israel for a year, giving her a significant knowledge advantage over me. I asked if we could discuss the beginning of the *parsha* of *Lech Lecha,* the third chapter in *Breishit* (Genesis). This is the momentous scene in which God directly instructs Avraham (Abraham) to leave everything behind and travel to a new, as yet unnamed land, where God promises to fulfill Avraham's destiny to become "a great nation." In this scene, Avraham is still known as Avram, and his wife is known as Sarai. Soon God will add the spiritually significant letter *hey* to both their names, and they will become known as Avraham and Sarah:

> "HaShem said to Avram, 'Go for yourself from your land, from your relatives, and from your father's house to the land that I will show you. And I will make of you a great nation; I will bless you, and make your name great, and you shall be a blessing. I will bless those who bless you, and him who curses you I will curse; and all the families of the earth shall bless themselves by you.'"

Rose and I each have a thick volume of the Five Books of Moses open in front of us. The Hebrew text is on the right-hand side of the page and the English translation is on the left. But the actual text of the Torah narrative extends only about a quarter of the way down the pages. Most of the space is devoted to rabbinic commentary on just these few sentences alone. Rashi's interpretation gets star billing directly under the Hebrew text, in his own script. The rest of the commentary has been culled and edited from a wide variety of the sages and sacred books, including the great commentators known as the Ramban, the Rashbam, and the Kli Yakar. The most recent among these sages lived many hundreds of years ago.

We agree that I will read first. I feel fully engaged, all my senses alert. I sit up straight and breathe in deeply. I can't believe how excited I am to learn this way. I want to read well and not flub anything up, and not have Rose think I read slowly (even though I do). I see that this is relatively simple Hebrew, and I begin: *"Vayomer HaShem el Avram lech lecha mei'artzecha u'mimoladtecha u'mibait aveecha . . .* "

I finish reading the short paragraph and feel a frisson of pleasure. I'm learning "inside," and Rose and I will try to peel back layers of mystery to find the revealed depths in this narrative.

"The question everybody seizes on," Rose says, "is why does it say *lech lecha*, 'go *for* yourself'? Who else would he be going for? The word *lecha* is superfluous. Why didn't HaShem just say '*go*?'"

I cannot read the Rashi script, but highlights of his commentary are in English, so I read those lines: "Rashi says the word '*lecha*' means that Avraham should go *for* his own good, and the 'good' is that he will become a great nation. He says that Avraham and Sarah will not have children if they stay in the land of Canaan."

"But '*lecha*' can also mean 'with yourself' or 'to yourself.' So the command could also mean that Avraham will discover who he really is by agreeing to this unexplained journey," Rose observes, consulting a different edition of the Torah that includes commentaries in addition to those in my book. "Ready for a mystical interpretation? According to Rabbi David of Lelov, *lech lecha* means that Avraham is taking a journey to his soul. As Rav Zushya said, 'When I get to heaven, they will not ask me, "Why were you not Moses?" They will ask me, "Zushya, why were you not Zushya?"' Avraham won't know who he is, or fulfill his potential, unless he leaves his land. He's going *for* himself, as well as *to* himself."

We go deeper into this idea of the nuances of meaning of the word "*lecha*," and I try to picture Avraham, the very first Jew and the full name of my firstborn son, Avi, wrestling with what it will mean to leave behind almost everything and everyone he has ever known for an uncharted journey. Did he believe he was going *for* himself or *to* himself? Rose and I also notice the repetition of the word "blessing" in the text, but at the rate we are discussing things we probably won't get to it tonight. Instead, we delve further into the idea of what it means to change direction in one's life, an idea that resonates with both of us. Before I know it a half-hour has zapped by, and we haven't even fully discussed two words! No wonder people can sit and study the Torah for years and years. There is so much to explore!

We decide to push on, hoping to at least complete the analysis of the whole sentence. Now we are in the thick of discussing why God phrased his instruction to Avraham to leave "from your land, from your relatives, and from your father's house . . ."

"That's not the order that one would think is normal," Rose says. "If you're going to move far away, aren't you first leaving your house and relatives and then, finally, leaving your country?"

I see a comment on this from the Ramban (13th century). "The order is in ascending levels of difficulty," I read. "It is hard for someone to leave his homeland, even harder to leave his extended family, and hardest of all to leave his parents." Even though I'm only reading the insights of someone else, I continue to experience the thrill of discovery with every sentence. I'm learning not just what Avraham went through in the process of becoming the first Jew, but gaining the Torah's insights into human psychology. Not bad at all for only an hour's investment of time.

"Think about that level of trust Avraham needed to have had when HaShem called to him to begin this journey," Rose suggests. "It was unnatural in the ancient world to just pick up like that and go. Avraham is expressing his free choice and free will to go against his society, which was filled with idol worship and the culture surrounding that ideology."

"Just like Jews have had to pick up and be ready to leave inhospitable lands through the generations," I observe.

"And just like *baalei teshuva* do–of course on a much, much lower level–when we decide to become observant when our family and friends are not. I'm sure you've heard that expression from the Talmud, 'Where a *baal teshuva* stands not even a perfect tzadik (righteous person) can stand,'" Rose says.

"Yes, my rabbi has said that, I think to help shore up our confidence. But that sounds pretty grandiose to me. I still don't do a lot of the mitzvahs fully, and some not at all, so I can't imagine myself anywhere near tzadik territory. But it's nice to know that our efforts to grow are valued so highly."

"It's a journey," she says. "No one does everything right."

The hour is up and the women are closing their books and

saying their goodbyes. There is still so much I'd love to discuss with Rose: Why so many repetitions of the word "blessing"? What did HaShem mean by making Avraham a 'great nation,' when we've always been numerically so tiny and always subject to hatred? Of course, I can read commentaries on all this on my own, but the team study session is very energizing.

I hope that this event, which was the first of its kind that I had heard of locally, continues. The depth of meaning I discover assures me, though I have long been convinced, that the Torah could only have been divinely authored. Studying Torah, especially "inside" the texts, gives me a tangible spiritual high. I am gaining precious wisdom that is coming in handy as a wife, mother, friend, writer, and in just about every sphere of life. Jeff and I anticipate facing significant challenges raising our children in today's complex and scary world, a world increasingly at odds with our values and vision. We are counting on this Torah wisdom to help guide us into the uncertain future.

Chapter 20

OUT IN THE WORLD

1993

I'M PUSHING A BIG RED SHOPPING CART AT TARGET, loaded with a cushy kitchen floor mat, jumbo bag of dog food, and dozens of other household and personal items I had no idea I needed till they were right in front of my face. At the intersection of the breakfast cereal aisle and the sturdy melamine dishes and cups aisle, a young man comes over to me. Somehow, he's holding on to a rolled-up outdoor carpet under one arm while hugging a large utility bin filled with kitchen knickknacks with the other arm. "Excuse me," he asks politely, "where can I find the nearest *keylim mikveh*?"

There are at least a hundred other shoppers at Target at this moment, but my outfit of below-the-knee denim skirt, three-quarter-sleeved shirt, and a beret alerts this shopper to the fact that I may be the only person in this enormous emporium–possibly in the entire zip code–who will know how to find what he's looking for: a mikveh used to immerse new dishes and cookware. I happily provide the intelligence and with enormous self-restraint suppress my urge to ask: "You couldn't get a cart?"

My "uniform" makes me a marked woman wherever I go. At the mall, the park, the theater, even in the great outdoors of Yosemite, other observant Jews spot me right away just as my radar detects their location coordinates from nearly a mile away. When I spot another long-sleeved Sister of the Tribe, our eyes lock for a second and we nod to one other almost imperceptibly, like a secret handshake. *I already know a lot about you*, we are each thinking, imagining similar frenzied Friday afternoons getting ready for Shabbos, shared juggling acts at work while also orchestrating the home front, coordinating carpool schedules, and perhaps wondering when we will finally manage to go out on a date night with our equally busy husbands. We are minorities within a minority, sharing a silent yet fundamental rapport.

Being publicly, identifiably Jewish can stir reactions from both Jews and non-Jews. Sometimes, Jews who are not ritually observant go out of their way to make sure that Orthodox Jews realize that they are Jewish too. Even if you're just standing in a line at a store, sitting in a waiting room, or networking at a professional event, a fellow Member of the Tribe (MOT) is apt to sashay over and offer a casual pleasantry, often tossing in a Hebrew or Yiddish word like a conversational wink. If it's Friday, the MOT might say, "I bet you're getting ready for *Shabbes*," using the Yiddish pronunciation and watching for your reaction. I love these opportunities to talk to other Jews who are outside my orbit, even for a few minutes. I'll smile and engage in conversation not just because I'm usually feeling friendly but because I want to show the MOTs that most Torah-observant Jews *are* friendly and open.

This is important public relations damage control because some Jews, who tend to live in the most insular Orthodox communities and fearful of the influences of secular society encroaching on their lives, can be decidedly unfriendly, even rude, to outsiders. Every time I hear about these incidents I feel both embarrassed and frustrated. Greeting others with a *seyver panim yafot*, (literally, the "expression of a nice face," one that conveys kindness) even people with whom we have had disagreements, is an important mitzvah. And you can't be "a light unto the nations" when you've got a dark, forbidding expression on your mug.

My friend Marc, whom I have known for years and have never seen without his *seyver panim yafot,* has even parlayed many of these chance encounters into meaningful friendships. In a Whole Foods Market, a hotel lobby, an airplane, or at his office, Marc is fortified not only with a his genuine and ready smile but also a pocketful of small cards that he has personally created containing bits of Jewish insights. Marc offers cards to anyone who seems receptive.

"Do you know the person you're dating?" asks one card on the front. On the other side, there is a list of ten clarifying questions to ask on a date. The front of another card asks the most famous question asked by Aish HaTorah founder Rabbi Noah Weinberg, "What are you living for?" On the other side, there is a simple exercise to help uncover the answer. Several young men and women whom Marc has met "at random" have ended up at their first-ever traditional Shabbos meals, hosted by Marc and his wife, Beth. Some have also gone to Marc's classes on relationships, taught in his home. I'm not as bold as Marc, but his caring and openness have led to hundreds of people finding friendship and a path to meaningful Jewish knowledge and living over the years. What a guy!

Sometimes, non-observant Jews like to ask questions about Orthodox Jewish practice or lifestyle. Once I tried out a "laughter yoga" class, just to get material for a column. As usual, my attire tipped off two other Jewish women in attendance that I probably haven't had a cheeseburger in a long time. When the class was over, the duo peppered me with questions and observations: they didn't think I could come to events like this, with men and women together. In fact, did I get out much at all? Did I grow up this way? (I love that phrase, "this way," as if Orthodoxy is a handicap I was born with, like a clubfoot.)

When they saw that I welcomed their questions, they went deeper, plunging forward with one that rattles many non-Orthodox Jews: "Isn't it true that Jews like you look down on Jews like us, who don't keep the Sabbath like you do? We're just as Jewish as you are!" one of the women said emphatically. (Oy, had I only known that laughter yoga was such a great place to do Jewish outreach I would have scooped up a bunch of Marc's cards and brought a whole bunch with me!)

I assured them that "Jews like me" did not look down upon them for not keeping the Sabbath. I told them that I myself hadn't kept Shabbos until my mid-twenties and have grown in my practice slowly. Jews are obligated to love their fellow Jews, not reject them, I said, though we do reject and judge certain actions that go against the Torah. They listened intently, and I hoped I was helping to mend, even a little bit, the rift that too often divides Jews along the observance spectrum. If Marc had been there he would have taken their numbers and invited them for Shabbos dinner the following week. But I didn't extend myself like I could have, and I lost the opportunity.

Most *baalei teshuva* have heard this same line, "We're just as Jewish as you are!" many times. Often, we are confronted by relatives who feel a little defensive that someone in their orbit is choosing to hew closer to tradition than the rest of the family. They may worry that the new *baal teshuva* may begin to feel superior to them. Or perhaps in some cases they worry that becoming more immersed in Jewish study and practice is contagious. It's easy to become smug, but it's an equal opportunity emotion: I've heard Orthodox Jews disparage the non-Orthodox for their flagrant disrespect of the Torah. I've also heard the non-Orthodox disparage the Orthodox for being insular and intolerant. Each side has work to do, not on "the others" but on ourselves.

Since I vividly remember the days when I used to slink low behind my steering wheel on Saturday while driving past smartly dressed Jews walking to shul, I understand both the insecurity and the annoyance. Back then I'd hear the little voice of my conscience asking, *Shouldn't you be out there walking to shul with them instead of going shopping? What if it all really does matter in the end?* Then I'd turn on the radio because I didn't want to hear any more.

Jews believe that the *Mashiach* (Messiah) has not yet come, but that God promised that he will, and then peace will finally reign throughout the world. Even among Jews! Given how contentious we can be as a people, peace among all Jews could only happen through an act of God. Until then, as Jeff likes to say, "Jews need to remember that what we have in common is greater than what divides us." Or as the seventh Lubavitcher Rebbe, Rabbi Menachem Mendel Schneerson, said regarding the term "Orthodox Judaism," "Splitting Judaism into 'orthodox, conservative and reform' is a purely artificial division, for all Jews share one and the same Torah given by the One and same God. While there are more observant Jews and less observant ones, to tack on a label does not change the reality that we are all one."

There is a concept from the Talmud known as the *pintele Yid*. This Yiddish phrase means "small Jew" but is meant to describe the spiritual core that lives in every Jew, no matter how removed that person might be from ritual practice or study. I think that it's the *pintele Yid* that sometimes motivates Jews to announce themselves as Jewish to an MOT wearing the "religious" uniform, and sometimes to confess to a depth of feeling for their heritage that they hadn't even realized was simmering inside.

I will never forget the day that my friend "Ellen" called me, nearly in tears. Days before, Ellen had just had her first child, a beautiful healthy son. I was very happy for her, as she married in her late thirties and very much wanted children. Ellen was Jewish but her husband, "Stephen," was not. She was stunned to discover after their son was born that Stephen was adamantly against having the baby circumcised. I had known Ellen for a few years, and while she didn't observe much Jewish practice, she had a real Jewish *neshama*, a Jewish soul. I was sad that she hadn't found a Jewish man to marry, but I did not judge her for the decision she made.

"Judy, I can't understand why I'm so upset by this. I don't keep Shabbos or kosher but I can't imagine having a son, a Jewish son, who isn't circumcised. I don't know what to do," she said, her voice filled with emotion. "Why do I feel this way?"

"Ellen, this is primal," I said. "The bris (circumcision) was the first covenant between a Jew and God, and it has become part of who we are–it's in our spiritual DNA. Maybe in a few days Stephen will have a change of heart when he sees how important it is to you." I hoped I was right. I was relieved when Ellen did call me several days after that to say that Stephen had relented. Their son did not have a Bris Milah ceremony (the covenant of circumcision) performed by a mohel, who has extensive training in making the ceremony safe and as painless as possible–but at least the baby was circumcised. Ellen's call made me realize that not just how I dressed but how I lived might become an invitation for other Jews to ask for my advice or for more knowledge about our traditions. It was both a responsibility and an honor.

Non-Jews notice us as well, and not infrequently comment on our modest dress. "I wish that more women dressed like you," a man called out to me when Jeff and I were about to go canoeing on a lake. Friends of mine have had similar experiences. At the Department of Motor Vehicles, where a friend had brought her daughter for her driver's test, the DMV employee helping them, an African-American man who appeared to be in his sixties, observed with a shake of the head, "If more girls covered up like you do we'd have a lot fewer problems between the boys and the girls." And another teenaged girl at the mall, dressed in "the uniform," came home and reported to her mother that one young man stared at her for a long time, making her very uncomfortable. The guy was probably not used to seeing young women preserving the mystery of their physical beauty, and discovered that mystery alluring.

Jeff's kippah is his most visible mark of religious observance, and we have been surprised yet pleased that so many of his customers view it as a sort of "*Good Housekeeping*" seal of approval or a kosher "branding" of sorts. (We also realize that the kippah might not engender this much enthusiasm in certain other areas of the country, less used to the sight of religious Jews.)

"I like that you wear that little beanie," a few customers have told Jeff. "I know you'll deal straight." The kippah is a Jewish man's reminder that there is always something over and above him—namely, God. Overall, we think it's been a bonus for business. Rarely, his kippah will awaken the inner anti-Semite of a person.

"No wonder your prices are so high. You Jews are only interested in money," Jeff's been told, suddenly finding himself on the defensive against the age-old stereotype. Fortunately, this has been a rare occurrence. I wish "the beanie" magically transformed all Jewish men into the kind of impeccably honest men they are supposed to be, but we are fallible human beings and have our share of scoundrels also. Their crooked ways create a *chillul HaShem*, a desecration of God's name that defames all of us. More than 2,000 years ago the sage Hillel famously explained to a would-be convert who demanded that he explain the entirety of Judaism while standing on one foot, "That which is hateful to you, do not do to your neighbor." Yes, that's where the Golden Rule comes from. But that was only the starting point. We were meant to refine ourselves much further from there.

I feel blessed to live in a time and a place where we can freely worship and go out in public dressed as identifiably Jewish, and not worry about anti-Semitism. This is decidedly not the case in much of the world, and it exists here, too, usually under the radar. Occasionally we will be out walking and some Jew-hating cretin will shout ugly expletives at us from a passing car, on a bicycle, or on foot. This is very unsettling, and a reminder that throughout history Jews have been reviled, envied, hated, beaten, killed, and kicked out of most countries where they had set down roots. Jeff and I suspect that our incredible freedom and safety as Jews in America won't last. Historically, it hasn't lasted anywhere in the diaspora for more than a few hundred years, so it's hard not to feel the clock is ticking here, too.

In our prayers every day we ask for God's protection from sickness, injury, accidents, evildoers, our own base inclinations, even litigants. (Leave it to the Jews to have such a comprehensive list of things to worry about.) But we also are constantly saying "thank you," and most of our prayers end with the word *Shalom*, which means both peace and wholeness. Blessings can only sprout from a foundation of peace.

As I choose my outfits each day and finesse the angle of my beret just so, I am also grateful for the opportunity–and the responsibility–of going out into the world, easily identifiable as a Jew.

Chapter 21

GRANDPA'S LITTLE GIRL

SPRING 1993

MOM AND I SAT IN THE HARD PLASTIC CHAIRS by his hospital bed, smiling weakly at him. We were waiting for results of a test that would confirm what we dreaded–that Dad had cancer. Mom and I sat quietly, hoping our presence would comfort him. There was little else we could do. Then Dad spoke.

"Judy, I was thinking how nice it would be if you had a little girl."

Well, this was a stunner. I had given birth to three boys in a little over four years. Avi was now four, Noah had recently turned three, and Ben was only ten months old. Of course, Dad loved his grandsons very much. Sometimes he drove all the way from Woodland Hills to Venice, a forty-minute trip each way, to pop over unannounced to see the boys.

"Little Benjamin," Dad would coo, rubbing noses with my youngest. "I love that name, Benjamin. Benjamin Isaac," he repeated, pronouncing Ben's full name as if it were a caress.

"And Little Noah and Big Avi!" Dad, otherwise known as

Grandpa, was supremely happy to watch them playing, and he laughed when Avi and Noah began roughhousing in their preschooler fashion. My sister Sharon had one son and one daughter, so Dad and Mom already had a legacy of five grandchildren to leave behind. Still, Dad and Mom had both made no secret of their worry about how far my unbridled fertility might go. Hours after Avi was born, Mom came to see us in the hospital. While she was happy, she still warned, "I hope you're not going to be back here next year with another one." I realized she was probably imagining me driving a huge Ford Club Wagon with my bounteous brood, and was concerned I'd wear myself out as a baby factory. I told myself that Mom's comment came from a place of love, but I barely managed to hold back my tears until she left.

At Avi's first birthday party, Dad was speaking to our good friend David, whose three youngest children stood near him. Dad said, "I think three children is enough for anybody, wouldn't you agree, David?" Dad asked.

David tilted his head ironically in his trademark style and gestured to his children. "These are my third, fourth, and fifth children. Which two should I not have had?"

Dad looked sheepish and embarrassed. Looking at the children, two of whom were devouring cupcakes and the other chomping on a cookie, he shrugged and said, "I guess I see what you mean."

Dad loved children, but I don't think he ever understood how anyone could support or take care of a large family, especially when he personally had struggled so much to make ends meet for us. In our community, with so many young married couples, new babies are always in various stages of production. Each birth is greeted with great rejoicing–and support. The *chesed* (kindness) committee springs into action, arranging for volunteers to bring dinners for the family for a full week after a new baby arrives, as well as for shopping and child care help. Of course, such care is there during sad times as well. This incredible care and practical assistance are what give so many of us the courage to continue to be fruitful and multiply like we do. In fact, Michael Medved likes to joke that the letters "PJC" don't stand for Pacific Jewish Center as much as they do *Prolific* Jewish Center.

"And here are the names I like best," Dad continued, deepening my amazement that he had thought this out so carefully. "Shoshana . . ." Mom and I agreed with him that Shoshana was a beautiful name.

"Naomi . . ." he continued, and again we nodded our approval.

"And my favorite: Muriel!" Dad smiled broadly. "Oh, how I love that name, Muriel."

"Muriel!" Mom and I laughed together. Dad's first two suggestions were popular in Jewish circles. But Muriel hadn't been trendy for probably forty or fifty years. It was such a funny moment at such a sorrowful time, but Dad's unprecedented discussion of a hoped-for granddaughter jarred me. Ever since Allan had died in that horrible car accident twenty-four years earlier, Dad had wanted nothing to do with God. I guess it was a family tradition: his father, Papa Rosenfeld, had forsaken God when his own father died during his childhood.

On the other hand, more than once, Dad had signaled his appreciation for the life Jeff and I were living. He never inquired about the whys and wherefores of what we did, nor did he ever attend synagogue with Mom; and he did not observe Shabbos or holidays, or keep kosher. But in another of Dad's trademark moments of doing the unexpected, on the Shabbos after our wedding, he asked for an audience to give a little impromptu speech–at shul. Both Jeff's and my parents had come to shul that day and would be joining us for the final meal of our *sheva brachos*, the series of celebratory feasts newlyweds are treated to during the week after the wedding. When the service was over and people began trooping to the upstairs balcony area where the refreshments of kiddush were served, Dad stood in the middle of the staircase and called for everyone's attention.

"Excuse me, ladies and gentlemen, I'd like your attention for a moment. May I please have your attention?" Jeff and I looked at one another in disbelief. Neither of us could imagine what in the world he was up to.

Dad didn't know anyone in the shul, and in fact had seen most of the members for the very first time at our wedding. "I just want to say on behalf of my wife, Liebe, and myself how much we appreciate the very warm welcome you have given us all. I'm not a religious man but I can see that the values that you all hold dear make this a very special group and special community. We know that Judy and Jeff will be very happy here. Thank you."

Dad was a big hit. While his articulation was a little muffled because of his severe hearing loss, his message was loud and clear. In a community of *baalei teshuva*, where nearly everyone had relatives who were perplexed or sometimes downright antagonistic to our choices, getting this sort of "huzzah" from a parent was a wonderful feel-good moment for us all. The men of the shul lined up to take turns shaking Dad's hand, thanking him, some of them hugging him. My eyes filled with tears to see this side of my father. He really was full of surprises.

Now, nearly six years later, Dad was peeling off another layer of a previously well-hidden spiritual side. I wondered whether God was somehow compensating for Dad's deteriorating physical condition by providing him with prophetic insights into my future.

Over the next eight months, my father slowly lost his battle with cancer, although he fought it with dignity and grace. I found in my father, forever wounded by Allan's loss, a kind of strength that I had not seen before, and my respect for him only grew. He never again spoke as he did that one day about my having another baby, but I never forgot his words. He had said it for a reason.

Several weeks before Dad passed away, I had a discussion with a friend named Robin, a rabbi's wife, about my observance of the laws of mikveh. Although I had used the mikveh regularly since Jeff and I had married, we had never made the extra effort to walk back from the ritual bath together on the infrequent occasions that my mikveh night fell on Shabbos or a holiday. Our home in Venice was four miles from the nearest ritual bath in Santa Monica, so for reasons of safety, convenience, and not wanting to fabricate a story for our children who would wonder why we were leaving when Shabbos was coming in, we held off until the next night when I could drive. We knew that our practice was somewhat compromised, and we were both increasingly bothered by our inconsistency. I mean, we didn't use "convenience" as an excuse to get out of other *mitzvot* we had accepted. As I suspected, Robin agreed.

"It's very, very important not to delay going to the mikveh," Robin said. "Mikveh is the spiritual foundation of the home. In fact, if a child is conceived after going to the mikveh on Shabbos, it's considered especially meritorious."

I reported this discussion to Jeff, and we agreed it was time to do this right. The next time my true mikveh night fell on a Friday or holiday, we'd not push it off any longer. Our newfound commitment was immediately put to the test. My next night to dip into the ritual bath fell on a Friday, so we hired our regular sitter and drove to the mikveh before candle lighting. Both of us had worn comfortable tennis shoes for the long walk home afterward.

Robin's words merged with Dad's prophecy. When I learned that I was expecting, I immediately felt that this was the little girl my father had spoken of. Exactly forty-eight hours after I learned that I was pregnant, Dad passed away peacefully in his sleep. Powerful emotions swept over me: grief, loss, and the surreal feeling that always accompanies the death of someone you loved very much.

At the same time, the promise of new life within me sustained me, a harmony linking life and death. I became convinced that my father had somehow known that I was destined to have a daughter.

Dad's wish came true. On February 16, 1994, our fourth child and first daughter was born. After three sons, we had a long list of girls' names that we liked, including Shoshana and Naomi. But we named her Yael, a name with significance on many levels. To honor Dad's memory, we took the letter *yud* from his Hebrew name, Yaakov. Yael is also a heroine from the book of Judges, a fearless woman who slew the vicious Canaanite general Sisera by hammering a tent peg into his head when he came into her tent looking for shelter. No, we didn't expect too much bloodshed among our four children, nor did we glorify violence, but we figured that a girl with three older brothers ought to know how to defend herself. The letter *yud* is also the smallest of the Hebrew letters, yet mystically alludes to HaShem's indivisible name. It also refers to the World to Come–the ultimate future.

Yael has a middle name also–Bracha, which means "blessing." Our journey had been rich with blessings since we'd begun it together six years earlier. We prayed that we would continue to experience them for many decades to come.

Chapter 22

SEVEN CIRCLES

DECEMBER 19, 2011

ALL FOUR KIDS ARE MUGGING FOR THE CAMERA, striking funny poses according to the photographer's direction. I'm standing by, highly amused, in my navy chiffon gown and pointy-toed stiff new shoes. In less than two hours Avi is getting married, and the photographer, our friend Jonah Light, is snap, snap, snapping away. He snaps as younger brothers Ben and Noah pick Avi up and hold him like he's a javelin that they're about to toss across the room, while Yael flashes the classic bemused expression of a little sister who has grown up amid the antics–and sometimes tyranny–of three older brothers. All together now, they are having a good time. They have outgrown most of the sibling rivalries and resentments from their childhood and teen years; anything that lingers is easily cast aside on this happy day.

The boys look so handsome in their suits, and Avi absolutely beams. Yael looks like a dream in her silver gown, impossibly high heels, and hair in an up-do. Jeff and I are *shepping* heaping servings of *Yiddishe nachas* today, reaping the quintessential Jewish joy of taking pride in our children's achievements. We are humbled by our incredible blessings. It has taken a long time to get to this point.

It is hard to believe that our eldest, just twenty-three, is getting married. Even harder to believe is that I actually picked Avi's wife for him, like my great-grandparents probably had done in a distant Eastern European town. When Avi had told us the year before that he was planning to use a *shadchan*, a matchmaker, to help him find that special young lady, I was less than thrilled. Many Orthodox singles use matchmakers. The best among the matchmakers get to know the young man or young lady they would like to set up and, with a minimum of wasted time and heartache, cull through their list of eligible prospects to find the most compatible candidates. Sometimes it works well; often, there is still a lot of wasted time and heartache. I still prefer the idea of singles meeting in more natural settings, such as at a Shabbos table, through friends, or even a singles mixer. But this isn't "done" in the circles that Avi has chosen to join.

"I know you better and love you so much more than any *shadchan* ever could," I had told him. "If you want to do it this way, fine, but I want to be involved in the process."

Avi agreed. Many months before he had planned to begin dating, a beautiful, bright, and charming twenty-year-old named Aliza waltzed right into my living room on the eve of Rosh Hashanah. She and her family were going to stay with us over the holiday. Avi was already living in New York, but at least for me, it was love at first sight. I had known Aliza's mother, Sharon, since the days we both lived in the Westwood Bayit, "way back in the day," as Avi would say, gesturing to the past with a sweep of his hand behind his head.

Sharon's life and mine followed parallel tracks. We each married and became more religiously observant. We started running into each other at the same little kids' birthday parties, discovering that three of our four children were very close in age. I couldn't understand why Sharon's husband, Manny, began to ask me if their family could sleep at our house over the High Holidays after they had moved to another neighborhood. They wanted to continue celebrating the Jewish New Year at the shul they used to attend and where we still belonged. But our house was not large, and we were each a family of six. Still, a few strategically placed sleeping bags and some kids doubling up did the trick. Years later, I get it: this match was *bashert*, or destined to happen.

Jeff and I never imagined that of all our kids, Avi would have chosen a more right-wing, *Yeshivish* form of Jewish observance. In fact, during his middle and high school years, he often appeared sullen and distant, both from us and from the Judaism we loved and had hoped all our children would love, too. As a teenager, he sometimes seemed lonely, and we worried that he might choose to peel away from Torah observance at the first opportunity. Too often, I needed antacids after our Shabbos dinners because Avi and Noah argued vehemently over points of Jewish observance and law, with Noah always defending tradition and Avi questioning tradition in a prickly fashion and staking out more liberal positions. No wonder the Torah shows us the first pair of brothers as mortal enemies, and the sons of all the patriarchs sometimes seething with animosity: these stories were a preview of coming attractions in our very own lives.

"Boys, *please* remember that we have so much more in common than what divides us," Jeff pleaded. But teenagers keep their deaf ears firmly planted for years. Would the two of them ever get along, we wondered? When would peace return to our Shabbos meals? We remained hopeful. We prayed a lot.

Jeff and I always knew that each of our kids would ultimately make their own decisions about whether to continue the path that we had charted. They might choose to be less observant than we were; they might choose to move further to the right. Our goal was to model, as best we could, both a loving marriage and the genuine excitement and enthusiasm we had for our Torah lives. As *baalei teshuva*, everything we were learning was new and fresh. Additionally, our choice to embrace tradition was a deliberate dissent from the declining culture around us. But our "*frum* from birth" kids (FFBs, for short) grew up with Torah practice as a given. They'd have to work harder than we did to retain that same appreciation and sense of discovery. As Jeff liked to say, they would each have to find a way to "make it their own." When Avi spent a year in Israel after high school, he decided to make Judaism his own, and he did it his way.

Robin, who stage-managed Jeff's and my wedding twenty-four years earlier, is organizing Avi and Aliza's wedding too. She comes to fetch me for the *bedecken*. Avi, Jeff, Noah, and Ben are off to the men's *tisch* (literally, "table") for singing, refreshments, and drinks, and a few legal preliminaries before the ceremony.

Sharon and I escort Aliza to her *bedecken* chair, accompanied by two clarinet-blaring musicians, playing "Od Yishama." My admiration and love for Aliza has grown even today, because after her makeup was on and she was getting into her gown, the zipper came undone completely–but Aliza didn't. A slightly panicked member of the bride's family burst into the room where Yael and I were having our makeup done and asked if anyone knew how to sew. My makeup lady said she did and dashed out to stitch my new daughter-in-law into her dress. At times like this, having faith really pays off.

As we sit on the raised platform, I look around the room and am filled with joy. So many of our dear friends from throughout our journey are here today; so many friends who danced at our wedding will soon dance with us again at the wedding of our son, including Sharon and David, and Carol and John, who flew out from New York. They have been like a second pair of parents to Avi.

Jeff and I stand not under the chuppah, but right outside it, looking in. Avi is in his new white *kittel*, standing next to his lovely Aliza. As the ceremony begins, they look at each other, smiling shyly. The man who has been our beloved rabbi for many years now, Rabbi Moshe Cohen, is tonight officiating at his first second-generation wedding; he performed Sharon and Manny's marriage ceremony, too. One by one people who have played instrumental roles in our families' lives come up for the honor of reciting one of the *sheva brachot*. When Rabbi Daniel Lapin comes up, he and I share a quick smile, capturing so many years of shared memories. At the end of the ceremony, Noah sings Psalm 128, which praises the virtues of love, family, and peace. He has a beautiful voice.

Jeff's parents are gone, as are mine. I know they must be watching and celebrating from *Olam Habah*, the World to Come, along with Nana and Papa, and even Cece and Papa, and all who came before from both sides of the family. When Avi crushes the glass with that satisfying stomp of his foot at the end of the ceremony, I can feel them joining in with the two hundred fifty people in the hall this evening who jump to their feet, shouting "Mazal tov!" and clapping and singing.

The atmosphere is electric–another "faithful house of Israel" is born.

Acknowledgments

Several years passed from the time the idea of this book first glimmered in my head till the time I completed it. For a few years I worked on the book in fits and starts until I realized I would never finish it unless I cleared away most other writing goals and focus fully on *The Skeptic and the Rabbi.*

I pressed many friends and family members into service, asking them to comment on the manuscript as it developed. I thank Linda Abraham, Martine Bellen, Robin Cantor-Cooke, Judith Cohen, Jessica Fauman, Rebecca Klempner, Denise Koek, Jessica Pishko, Richard Rabkin, and Gil Weinreich for their recommendations and encouragement. Each person brought something valuable to the critiquing table.

Sunny Cherme Cooper and Jennifer Lawler became close advisors in later stages, offering excellent guidance and direction that allowed me to further shape and sharpen my story. They are expert editors and became vital sources of moral support, believing in this book and boosting my confidence when it began to flag. I hope they will get a little *nachas* from seeing it completed, now that they know what this Yiddish word means!

Rabbi Nechemia Coopersmith and Richard Rabkin have been my editors at Aish.com for many years. I thank them for providing me so many opportunities to share my writing with such a valuable and enthusiastic readership.

The crack team at She Writes Press has been thoroughly professional, taking care with every step of the editorial, design, and production process. Thank you so much Brooke Warner, Cait Levin, Julie Metz and Lauren Wise. Niva Taylor's expert finishing touches on the manuscript and Stu Schnee's diligent publicity efforts are both much appreciated..

For questions on points of Jewish law and accurate representations of Jewish philosophy, I consulted Rabbi Moshe Cohen, our family rabbi for many years, as well as my sons, Avi, Noah, and Ben. Any errors in the text are my own.

Heartfelt thanks to Rabbi Daniel Lapin and his wife, Susan, for allowing me to parlay our years together in the PJC community, and my treasured friendship with them, into this story. No words can ever adequately express the thanks that Jeff and I will always have to both of you for taking us "newbies" by the hand, metaphorically speaking, and opening up the world of Torah to us.

My family has lived with this book project, and the angst and sleepless nights it often caused me, for a long time. No book that I could ever write is as important to me as being a wife and mother to the Gruen family. Thank you Jeff, Avi and Aliza, Noah, Ben and Rivka, and Yael and Yonah for your stalwart encouragement. Extra special thanks to Noah, a gifted writer, for having reviewed the manuscript multiple times, always finding meaningful improvements.

As Jewish tradition teaches, we save the most precious for last. I thank the Almighty for my family and my health, gifts I enjoy every single day. I thank Him for guiding me to live a Torah life–a life of clarity, meaning, and inspiration.

About the Author

photo credit: Jonah Light

Judy Gruen's essays and features have appeared in media outlets including the *Wall Street Journal, Chicago Tribune, Boston Globe, Christian Science Monitor, Los Angeles Times, Saturday Evening Post, Jewish Journal, Jewish Action, Woman's Day, Family Circle,* and ten anthologies. A former columnist for Religion News Service, she is a frequent contributor to Aish.com. She lives in Los Angeles with her husband, Jeff.

READER'S GUIDE

The Skeptic and the Rabbi by Judy Gruen

DISCUSSION QUESTIONS

1. Who are the skeptic and the rabbi in this story? In the beginning, it seems the author is the skeptic and Rabbi Lapin is the rabbi. Who else fulfills these roles in her story? Does the author herself ever become the rabbi?
2. The author's "wildly divergent" grandparents–the Cohens and the Rosenfelds–reflect the dueling tension between her family's identities: secular versus religious. The author longs to find a happy medium, the "best of both worlds." Do you think she resolved this tension? Why or why not?
3. Early in the story, the author fears that a Torah-based lifestyle will be anti-feminist and antiquated. What were the key turning points that convinced her otherwise? Was it a complete or only partial transformation of belief?
4. This book has a lot of humor, both self-deprecating humor as well as about Orthodox practice itself. What impact did comedic elements have on the narrative? What are some of the most memorable humorous moments for you?
5. When the author finally agrees to meet Rabbi Lapin and attend his class, she knows she has gone further than she had ever

intended in exploring Jewish Orthodox tradition. Did you feel her reactions to the rabbi and his class were authentic? Did it seem that she was forcing herself to go along for the sake of her romance with Jeff?

6. Rabbi Lapin's teachings about the importance of tradition both unsettle and also resonate with the author. She is struck when at one point he says, "Without living links to the past and to the future the present lacks vitality." Do we too easily throw off the values of the past in today's society?
7. During her spiritual search, the author worries about changes she will have to make in her life, such as no longer shopping on Saturdays and possibly losing some friends. Do her changes feel like significant sacrifices? Does she express remorse or regret over them?
8. The death of the author's brother, Allan, and its emotional and spiritual aftermath, haunt her for many years. What impact, if any, do you feel this loss had on her ultimate decision to embrace Orthodoxy?
9. Once the author places her bet on the life of "rules, rituals, and restraints" as outlined in the Orthodox Jewish community she has embraced, she finds herself in awkward and embarrassing situations that trigger her insecurities again. What were some of these moments? Did you relate to any of these situations?
10. The trip to the Soviet Union seemed to solidify the author's commitment to her Cohen grandparents' worldview. Scenes of Judy meeting her Russian family in the airport, being feted with a luxurious feast in their small apartment, and standing alone before a locked synagogue door, paint vivid portraits of personal, family, and cultural Jewish history. Which scenes from that chapter most resonated with you?

11. In comparison to other contemporary Jewish memoirs, such as *All Who Go Do Not Return* by Shulem Deen and *Unorthodox: The Scandalous Rejection of My Hasidic Roots* by Deborah Feldman, what is the driving message of Gruen's memoir?

12. Gruen has touched on themes of feminism, logic, faith, and family in her memoir. Do you feel she has thematically resolved her spiritual journey for herself?

13. In Chapter 20, Gruen writes about how it feels to be out in the world, obviously marked by her clothing and hair covering as an Orthodox Jewish woman. This triggers both positive and sometimes antagonistic comments from non-Orthodox people. What skeptics does Judy encounter, and how does she respond to this underlying or overt tension? How often do we encounter people who are deeply unsettled by our own beliefs?

14. In the same chapter, the author quotes the late Chabad Lubavitcher Rebbe, saying, "There is no such thing as an Orthodox Jew, or a Conservative Jew or Reform Jew. We are all Jews, period." After reading this book, how does this quote resonate with you? Have any stereotypes been cleared up? What questions or impressions are you left with?

15. In today's 24/7 wired society, does the idea of a traditional Sabbath–a day of "being and not doing," including turning off computers and smartphones–resonate? Why or why not?

16. Is Judy still a feminist at the end of the story? Why or why not? Is it important for a modern woman to identify as a feminist?

SELECTED TITLES FROM SHE WRITES PRESS

She Writes Press is an independent publishing company founded to serve women writers everywhere. Visit us at www.shewritespress.com.

Renewable: One Woman's Search for Simplicity, Faithfulness, and Hope by Eileen Flanagan. $16.95, 978-1-63152-968-9. At age forty-nine, Eileen Flanagan had an aching feeling that she wasn't living up to her youthful ideals or potential, so she started trying to change the world–and in doing so, she found the courage to change her life.

Accidental Soldier: A Memoir of Service and Sacrifice in the Israel Defense Forces by Dorit Sasson. $17.95, 978-1-63152-035-8. When nineteen-year-old Dorit Sasson realized she had no choice but to distance herself from her neurotic, worrywart of a mother in order to become her own person, she volunteered for the Israel Defense Forces–and found her path to freedom.

Motherlines: Letters of Love, Longing, and Liberation by Patricia Reis. $16.95, 978-1-63152-121-8. In her midlife search for meaning, and longing for maternal connection, Patricia Reis encounters uncommon women who inspire her journey and discovers an unlikely confidante in her aunt, a free-spirited Franciscan nun.

This Trip Will Change Your Life: A Shaman's Story of Spirit Evolution by Jennifer B. Monahan. $16.95, 978-1-63152-111-9. One woman's inspirational story of finding her life purpose and the messages and training she received from the spirit world as she became a shamanic healer.

Uncovered: How I Left Hassidic Life and Finally Came Home by Leah Lax. $16.95, 978-1-63152-995-5. Drawn in their offers of refuge from her troubled family and promises of eternal love, Leah Lax becomes a Hassidic Jew–but ultimately, as a forty-something woman, comes to reject everything she has lived for three decades in order to be who she truly is.

Change Maker: How My Brother's Death Woke Up My Life by Rebecca Austill-Clausen. $16.95, 978-1-63152-130-0. Rebecca Austill-Clausen was workaholic businesswoman with no prior psychic experience when she discovered that she could talk with her dead brother, not to mention multiple other spirits–and a whole new world opened up to her.